COMEDY OF DOOM

BY JOSEPH SCRIMSHAW

Joseph Scrimshaw

JOKING ENVELOPE

Joseph Scrimshaw is a writer and comedian who was once described by a fan on Twitter as "geek flavored."

As a "geek flavored" comedian, he's performed at the San Francisco SketchFest, Chicago Improv Festival, CONvergence, H.P. Lovecraft Film Festival, Jonathan Coulton's JoCoCruiseCrazy, and more.

He's written for RiffTrax, John Kovalic's Dork Storm Press, and the Minnesota Public Radio show *Wits*. His hit plays *Adventures in Mating, The Worst Show in the Fringe, An Inconvenient Squirrel*, and *My Monster* (written with Bill Corbett) have been performed all over the world.

Joseph also has a podcast about liking things a little too much called *OBSESSED (With Joseph Scrimshaw)*. The podcast features comedy monologues, rants, and guest interviews, all recorded with a live audience.

In his free time, Joseph plays the drums, spends an obsessive amount of time on Twitter, and enjoys watching his wife knit.

To contact Joseph, follow his Twitter account (@JosephScrimshaw), listen to his podcast, buy Joseph-related things, or, to look at a picture of Joseph cosplaying a squirrel, visit www.josephscrimshaw.com.

OTHER WORKS BY JOSEPH

PLAYS AVAILABLE FOR PURCHASE

Adventures in Mating

An Inconvenient Squirrel

The Worst Show in the Fringe

Fat Man Crying

Stitch, Bitch N' Die

COMING SOON

Sexy Librarian: File Under Rock Musical
Music by Mike Hallenbeck

The Damn Audition

Brain Fighters

Nightmare Without Pants

BOOKS JOSEPH MIGHT WRITE IN THE FUTURE

Jokes To Make Love By: A Coffee Table Book with Glossy Photos

Five Out of The Seven Habits Of Highly Effective Procrastinators

*I Know Why The Caged Bird Drinks:
Poems About Spirits*

*Married With Benefits:
A Guide To Letting Your Wife Get You Health Insurance*

*A Small Book Collecting Tweets
I Feel Could Have Been Retweeted More*

*What's Wrong With Me That All My Book Titles Are So Damn Long?:
An 8000 Page Essay on Navel Gazing*

This book is dedicated to my wonderful wife, Sara Stevenson Scrimshaw.

Also, squirrels.

Not only did my wife encourage me to write this book, she understands my sense of humor so well she won't be even remotely offended that she is sharing a dedication with a species of rodents.

Copyright © 2012 by Joseph Scrimshaw.

All rights reserved. No part of this publication may be reproduced, distributed, or transmitted in any form or by any means, including photocopying, recording, or other electronic or mechanical methods, without the prior written permission of the publisher, except in the case of brief quotations embodied in critical reviews and certain other noncommercial uses permitted by copyright law. Please contact the publisher for all permission requests.

Published by Joking Envelope, LLC. Minneapolis, MN. www.jokingenvelope.com

Manufactured in the United States of America.

ISBN-13: 978-0-9856856-0-7

TABLE OF CONTENTS

Introduction of Doom *by Bill Corbett* 1

Foreward of Doom 5

Origin of Doom 11

Dungeons & Dragons & You 17

Emotional Preparation for the Zombie Apocalypse 19

Me Like Tacos 25

Word Porn 27

A Brief TED Talk 31

A Death Star to Guide Me 33

The Sensitive Generation 39

For Your Expense Report Only 41

So Much Luke 51

The Thing That Should Not Be Under Your Bed
illustrations by John Kovalic 53

A Public Service Announcement 63

Super Mario Subtext 65

A Legitimate Superhero Suggestion 71

A Complete Guide to Competitive Hugging 73

A Different Perspective on Cat Pictures 87

The Real-Life Adventures of Murder Master 9000 89

A Terrible Bat-Epiphany 99

Sense and Seven Minutes in Heaven 101

The Doom from the '70s 109

The Wrath of Humanity 111

The Ides of March 117

A Song of Rainbows and Also Rainbows. 119

Thinking Outside the Brain 123

Curse of the Naked Mime *illustrations by Joseph Scrimshaw* 125

A Word Problem 135

You Are an Awful Human Being! 137

A Dangerous Mistake 157

The Honey Bear Rises *illustration by Christopher Jones*. 159

Hours of Creepy Fun. 173

Bullshit Time 175

A Pants-Based Goal 181

The Indirect Advice of Utter Uselessness 183

Idiot Mode. 193

Spaceship Whatever Something GO! 195

Literature with Emoticons. 199

Blink Blink Blank. 201

Dystopian Kegger 209

Date Night (in Mind-Blowing 3D) 211

Free Advice about Life 215

Internet Comments of a Sad Vampire 217

Schrödinger's Joke. 225

An Old Hope. 227

Conclusion of Doom. 237

Geek Topics Covered Index. 241

Geek Topics Missed 243

Hall of Gratitude 247

Thanks of Doom 249

"He keeps asking me to write a play about the Bataan Death March. I keep telling him, 'Okay, but I'm going to write it as a comedy.' That's just how it makes sense to me."

—Tom Poole, playwright, giver of good advice, lover of comedy

"From now on, I'm going to put everything I say in quotes to give it more of a sense of history and weight."

—Joseph Scrimshaw, jackass who writes inspirational quotes for the beginning of his own book

INTRODUCTION OF DOOM

LADIES AND GENTLEMEN, MY FRIEND JOSEPH SCRIMSHAW IS A MAN OF many talents. Let there be no doubt about that! He is a brilliant writer and performer, as anyone who has ever seen him write, perform, or DO BOTH AT ONCE can attest.

(Seriously, I once saw him performing the part of Malvolio in *Twelfth Night*, hilariously, WHILE writing a moving epic poem on the Spanish Civil War. You didn't even notice that "Malvolio" was writing furiously as he minced uproariously about the stage, and yet—by the time curtain call came around—Joseph had in hand a 150-page masterpiece about the courage of the Lincoln Brigade, done in perfect Spenserian stanza. It was like the best, artsy-fartsiest magic trick ever.)

But Joseph's résumé boasts of even more than that! For example, his line of artisanal lingonberry jams in thirty-seven different varieties and counting (though all lingonberry-based). His résumé also brags of discovering and naming thirty-seven new species of weevil, and of his killing thirty-seven evil henchmen with his trusty thirty-seven–inch katana in thirty-seven minutes.

Yes, these boasts are nonsense with a strange numerical obsession. We are not sure yet whether it is Joseph himself lying or that his résumé has come to sudden sentience and is prone to compulsive boasting. But we shouldn't let this obscure the fact that Joseph is a phenomenally talented man!

More seriouswise: I have had the pleasure of collaborating with Joseph on a bunch of projects, and he never fails to impress me all over again with the range of his tremendous talents. We created a few live pieces together and they were some of the most fun I've ever had onstage.

(And I say "live pieces" because, true to the destiny he and I share—or are cursed with—they were both some hybrid of sketch comedy, stand-up, theater, storytelling, and ultimate fighting. We are cross-genre freaks, pity us!)

In this collection of Joseph's writing, you get a sense of what makes his funny, fevered brain work. There's a lot of geekery to be sure: video games, *Star Wars*, and other straight-from-geek-central topics that Joseph considers smartly and then goes beyond the usual nerd analysis with the sheer power ("Force") of his wit. To take just one example, here's his description of the *Doctor Who* theme:

> "Suddenly the opening credits come on. You are flying down a tunnel. It's disturbingly similar to the video you saw in health class of a camera traveling through a urethra. The music is creepy, cool, and funny all at the same time, like if Al Yankovic wrote the music for your funeral."

That passage not only made me L, my friends. I also did it O L! (Though I did not R O T F, because I am too old and might never get up, instead gradually mutating into a creepy throw rug with vestigial eyeballs.)

So now that I have quoted a passage from Joseph's book, you may be delighted to find out that this very book IS that book and that very passage is contained within. PLUS there is more writing than that! Yes, it's not just a fifty-word book like most stuff on the market! There's a lot more wit, wisdom, and something else that starts with *wi-* inside. Windmills? Wisconsin? Will.i.am? This is yours to discover because I have not done it for you! Sorry!

And with that, I wish you great enjoyment as you traipse through the comedic mind of Joseph Scrimshaw. So pull on your mental fishing waders, step into the rushing waters of his turbulent genius, and somehow complete my metaphor.

Enjoy *Tragedy of Hope* (right? I don't have time to check the title. That might not seem to make sense until you realize that I am in a cliffside trap set by Joseph which was designed to push me into the Arctic Ocean in five minutes if I didn't write a book intro that pleases him and— aefq347t1yfska[eigj3

Bill Corbett
Writer/Performer/Clownhunter

May 29, 2012

FOREWARD OF DOOM

I WOULD LIKE TO CONGRATULATE YOU ON YOUR PURCHASE, BORROWING, theft, or discovery in a time capsule of this book.

Comedy of Doom is a comedy book that is not actually full of doom, but a bunch of stuff relating to the wide world of geek. Geek, as a word, is pretty difficult to pin down. Merriam-Webster offers these fun options:

> *geek:* A carnival performer often billed as a wild man whose act usually includes biting the head off a live chicken.
>
> *geek:* A person often of an intellectual bent who is disliked.

Wikipedia offers even more descriptions:

> Some geeks have cultivated a geek culture, such as obscure references on t-shirts.
>
> A geek is a person who relates academic subjects to the real world; for example, using multivariate calculus to determine how they should correctly optimize the dimensions of a pan to bake a cake.

So in theory, this book deals with topics that will be interesting to intelligent chicken biters who use calculus to bake cakes while wearing funny t-shirts and being disliked.

I don't really have a lot of material for that book. This would be the whole thing:

> Hey, look at that genius! Baking a chocolate cake with numbers and spilling chicken blood on one of those *Star Track* t-shirts! Way to multitask, you jackass!

I didn't want to write that book, so I gave some thought to what the word "geek" means to me. To me, the word "geek" is sort of like Luke Skywalker going into the dark cave on Dagobah in *The Empire Strikes Back*. The only things it means are the things you bring with you.

Personally, I think a geek is an intelligent person who likes something, often obsessively, and is not afraid to be really loud about it. Geeks can be obsessive about anything: television shows, movies, trains, books, chicken biting, sports, cake, pie, pi, needlepoint, video games, lists, and maybe even lists that use Oxford commas.

The other important factor in my personal definition of "geek" is, for lack of a better term, a sense of mental adventure. The origin story of most geeks is seeing something that other people don't.

Instead of a silly TV show with crappy special effects, geeks can see a different universe. Instead of a pile of yarn, geeks can see an ironic sweater vest. Instead of just a couple of computers hooked together with tubes, geeks can see a virtual reality where we can show one another pictures of our cats almost instantaneously.

So while I see being a geek as somewhat of a perspective or state of mind, there is certainly a collected body of knowledge that many geeks share.

I call this collected body of geek knowledge NERDLORE.

There are plenty of people out there who are awfully geeky about cars or history who would be alarmed to find themselves at a convention full of people yelling things like:

Han shot first!

The cake is a lie!

or

I'm going to squee!

More on squeeing later.

To my geek readers who perhaps only know enough nerdlore to order a drink and ask for directions to the bathroom, I apologize. That reference to Luke entering the dark cave was probably pretty confusing. It was just a nerdlore way to say soul searching. (Plus, a head got cut off in the cave so it had thematic resonance with the chicken biting.)

In spirit, I intend this book for geeks of all kinds—intelligent, passionate people who have an open mind about becoming obsessed with something new.

In practice, some stories include straight-up nerdlore. If you aren't sure what something means, just look it up on the computer tubes for the cat viewing or ask someone with an obscure reference on their t-shirt. Perhaps you will learn something new to impress or confuse your friends!

And speaking of learning, I made a lot of personal discoveries as I assembled this book. Some of the stories come from my live comedy shows, a few from my dream journal, a few from my podcast, and many are brand new. Many of them focus on the traditional nerdlore canon while others tackle my own personal geekery.

As I pulled it all together I realized that certain themes and topics kept rearing their ambiguous heads. Not nerdlore topics like *Doctor Who* or superheroes. I knew I would be tackling those. (They are lovingly catalogued at the end of every piece under "Geek Topics Covered.")

No, the topics that came up are clearly little obsessions of mine. I suggest you deal with them the same way I do: by laughing and having a drink.

Here's a brief guide to the official *Comedy of Doom* drinking game:

1. Every time there is swearing, take a drink.
2. Every time there is fake swearing, take a drink.
3. Every time I mention my mother, take a drink.
4. Every time there is a particularly optimistic passage, take a drink.
5. Every time there is a particularly pessimistic passage, take a drink.
6. Every time frozen pizza is mentioned, take a drink.
7. Every time there is drinking, take a drink.
8. Every time you laugh then spill your drink on the book, get another drink.

And if you spill on the book, don't worry. It will give the book more character. Unless you're reading this on a phone or a tablet. Then you're kind of screwed.

Before I send you off to get totally hammered reading my book, I need to return to the issue of squeeing. Squeeing is a short, emphatic nerdlore term for almost unbearable excitement. I'm all for the emotion and the expression, I just can't get behind the word choice.

When I hear the word "squee," I picture a panel from a *Star Wars* comic book in which R2-D2 is farting—big, block letters shooting from the little astromech droid's backside. As much as I appreciate the emotion, I can't bring myself to say, "I really enjoy the comedy of Bill Corbett. I think I'll use my mouth to fart like a robot."

So while I really do want you to have many delightful squeeing moments while reading my book, I suggest these alternative noises: "Wuaaahhh!", "Shaaaaaadd!", or even a simple "HEYYYY-OOOOO!"

Finally, thank you very, very much for your time and your interest. The book will only get better from here, so sit back, relax, grab a drink, and enjoy.

Cheers,
Joseph Scrimshaw

P.S. That last sentence mentioned drinking, so you should probably take a drink.

1
ORIGIN OF DOOM

I WOULD LIKE TO INTRODUCE YOU TO MY FAVORITE TELEVISION SHOW exactly as it was introduced to me. Imagine one day, your older brother tells you this guy at school says there's an awesome science fiction show that plays every Friday and Saturday night on the *Sesame Street* channel.

You had no idea the *Sesame Street* channel even broadcast after 10 a.m., but you and your brother stay up late and tune in. Like literally tune in. You have to turn a PHYSICAL dial and adjust AN ANTENNA. Like you're a steampunk or something.

Suddenly the opening credits come on. You are flying down a tunnel. It's disturbingly similar to the video you saw in health class of a camera traveling through a urethra. The music is creepy, cool, and funny all at the same time, like if Al Yankovic wrote the music for your funeral. Then you watch as monsters come on the screen. Monsters outfitted with guns, toilet plungers, and bumps that look like the robot version of an STD outbreak. They match wits with a charming man whose nose is so large he would not be allowed on American television unless he was playing a serial killer or perhaps a defense attorney.

You watch again on Saturday night and see an entirely different charming man with an entirely different giant nose.

And you wonder: *What the hell is this?*

You want to look it up on Wikipedia. But Wikipedia doesn't exist yet. So you ask your brother to ask that guy he knows at school. Which when you think about it, isn't that different from looking it up on Wikipedia.

On Monday, you finally get the information download. The show is called *Doctor Who*. The plunger monsters are Daleks and the charming men with the giant noses are the Doctor. He's played by different actors because instead of dying like a boring American hero, he regenerates. He flies through time and space in a blue box because that seemed like a good idea to someone in 1963 and it never changed because, dammit, they like it that way.

So do you.

Your life is now changed. Every kid you know likes *Star Wars* and superheroes. But this is a low-budget, sometimes blatantly educational show featuring women whose breasts are often fully covered and a protagonist who actively tries to prevent cool military guys from blowing crap up. You will not be playing *Doctor Who* on the playground.

As a more pessimistic Obi-Wan Kenobi might say, "You have taken your first step into a much smaller world."

I took that step. I jumped off the cliff like a lemming with mild astigmatism.

I convinced my pals at school to give the show a try. They returned with this actual quote: "That show is so stupid, if you keep watching it, it will probably give you AIDS." It was a bit of a rough school with an obviously poor sex-ed program, but the kids were cool. I had always been a little weird, a little artsy, but the kids at this school liked and/or tolerated me. Then we moved to a different neighborhood with fancier schools. And against my will, I was forced to regenerate.

At the new school I was treated as a full-blown geeky loser. We had a reading period every day. The other kids brought sports magazines. They looked at the pictures and occasionally sounded out the captions. I brought novelizations of obscure *Doctor Who* episodes carefully wrapped in plastic comic book bags so the corners of the book wouldn't get bent. The bullies were so hypersensitive to people being different, they were already pissed off that I could even spell PBS. But a British science-fiction book in a plastic bag? That was like an attack on Middle America. I might as well have just stood up on a chair screaming, "Football sucks and your mothers all want to have sex with illegal immigrants!"

Against all normal instincts of self-preservation, I persisted in my *Doctor Who* love. When Halloween rolled around I dressed up as the Doctor's archenemy: The Master, an evil genius clad in ominous dark robes and gloves. The best I could do was faded black jeans, a black short-sleeved shirt with a little alligator in the corner, and one sparkly, white Michael Jackson glove. I spent the day repeating the Master's catchphrase, "I am the Master and you will obey me."

In retrospect, telling prepubescent girls to obey me was a little creepy. But I digress.

My conflict with the bullies culminated during a field trip to the Minnesota State Capitol. While standing in line, one of the bullies entertained himself with the stupidest of all bullying techniques, the tapping game.

He would tap me on the shoulder. I would turn around. He would look the other way. And repeat. It was as if he were preparing himself for the monotonous factory job he no doubt holds today.

TAP.

I had resisted getting into a physical fight all year because I wanted to be a pacifist like the Doctor.

TAP.

The Doctor would try to talk it out.

TAP.

I had tried but it didn't work.

TAP.

I admired the Doctor for his kindness and his empathy.

TAP.

But I also admired his willingness to fight.

TAP.

The only thing bigger than the Doctor's nose was his

brass fucking Time Lord balls.

TA—

I whirled around and punched the bully in the face. He punched me in the gut. I desperately tried to kick him in the crotch as the teacher pulled us apart. He, of course, mocked me for the rest of the year but never within punching range. And if I suddenly turned around and stared at him, he would flinch. I had triumphed!

What's more, I triumphed exactly the way the Doctor so often did: with just enough justifiable violence to hang on to the pacifist cred.

The next year I went to a different school and regenerated back into an artsy kid who was just kind of weird.

For better or worse, *Doctor Who* helped make me the man-child I am today. The show reminded me to value intelligence, creativity, poor fashion choices, and absolute pig-headed defiant individuality.

Over the years, I internalized my own inner *Doctor Who* novelization and lovingly wrapped it in plastic so the corners wouldn't get bent. If there were an inscription on the inside cover it would read:

I am Joseph Scrimshaw. I am my master and I will obey me.

GEEK TOPICS COVERED

▫ *Doctor Who* ▫ *Star Wars* ▫ Superheroes ▫ Steampunk
▫ Cosplay ▫ Wikipedia ▫ Al Yankovic ▫ Astigmatism

2
DUNGEONS & DRAGONS & YOU

Parents! Don't worry! Satan no longer speaks to your children through *Dungeons & Dragons,* but only because he thinks the new edition sucks ass.

GEEK TOPICS COVERED
❐ *Dungeons & Dragons*   ❐ Satan

3

EMOTIONAL PREPARATION FOR THE ZOMBIE APOCALYPSE

IF WISHING MAKES IT SO, THERE IS LITTLE DOUBT WE WILL SOON FACE the horror of a zombie apocalypse.

Many people consider themselves well prepared.

We all have our preferred zombie hunting weapons: shotguns, cricket bats, golf clubs, longbows, a replica of a broadsword from any one of the *Highlander* films or television series. Basically anything that is long and hard and might fire a projectile. That's normal and healthy. More on that later.

We all know where we would hole up to make our stand against the undead horde: Walmart, Kmart, Big K, Target, SuperTarget, Costco. Basically any location that has a lot of food and would also be a depressing place to die. That's just common sense. More on that later.

We all know who we would try to rescue and protect: our significant others, our children, quiet neighbors who keep to themselves because they probably have a lot of weapons in their basement. Basically all of the important people in our lives who are still mobile or have tactical value. Grandparents are pretty much out of luck. That's just good strategy. More on that later.

Say what you will about the lazy human beings of the 21st century, we are physically prepared for the zombie apocalypse. But at the risk of sounding unmanly, what about our feelings?

Are we as a people *emotionally* prepared for a zombie apocalypse?

Let's start by reconsidering some of our cold, cruel, and emotionally distant physical preparations.

Do we have to slaughter zombies with phallic objects? What if we imagine hitting them with something soft and beautiful? A tulip? A handwritten letter? An unframed Monet print from a college dorm room? Would that be effective? Probably not. Does it make you sad that beauty is useless against zombies?

What if we didn't make our final stand in a soulless big-box store? What if we went to a happy place? A used bookstore? A locally owned homeopathic day spa? A patch of shade under our favorite tree? Would these be good fortresses? Probably not. Does it upset you to know your happy places make for great zombie feeding grounds?

What if we didn't just rescue helpful people we love? What if we went out of our way to help a stranger? Or someone we knew to be a jerk? What if we raced to a nursing home to protect the older generation from certain doom? Would a cranky, wizened old man with a catheter and a penchant for racist slurs be a cheerful and valiant comrade for our desperate final stand? Of course not. Does it agitate you to think zombies might force you to die in the company of annoying people?

Zombies limit our options. And it makes us angry. It makes us want to kill them viciously in a large, well-lit retail environment.

Picture it: A reanimated heathen monstrosity shambles through SuperTarget. It's Doug. Doug from that yellow house down the street. He gives out full-size Snickers bars on Halloween, not just the misleadingly named fun-size. Doug is following you down the cleaning supplies aisle, his grisly arms outstretched as if asking for a reassuring hug.

You savagely beat him about the head with a metal toilet plunger designed by Michael Graves until his skull caves in like a rotten melon.

Achievement unlocked! You just killed (or re-killed) Doug, the full-size Snickers man from down the street! It's just like Xbox Live, but actually live!

How do you feel about murdering Doug? He made you do it, right?

But still…

Those are Doug's brains you splattered all over the cleaning supplies aisle. You'll be thinking about that when you get out that pole with the tennis ball on the end to rub the streaks off the cold, unforgiving tile. And as you stare at your reflection in the SuperTarget floor, the horrifying truth wrestles its way into your conscious mind: ZOMBIES ARE US.

On some level, we are the undead and the undead are us.

And so we have to ask:

Why are we hitting ourselves?

Why are we hitting ourselves?

Why are we hitting ourselves in a SuperTarget with a metal toilet plunger designed by Michael Graves?

Yes, the zombies make us do it. Yes, it's us or them. Yes, zombies are murderous mockeries of our former selves—mindless, unreasonable symbols of death and decay. But they do have one thing going for them:

Zombies are goal oriented.

Zombies want to eat the brains of the living and that is all. No excuses, no bullshit.

Zombies don't stand around at cocktail parties claiming they're going to eat brains after they go back to school and get their MFA in theoretical brain eating.

Zombies don't order copies of *Brain Eating for Dummies*

from Amazon then tell themselves they can start eating brains as soon as they get around to reading up on it.

Zombies don't drop everything and move across the country because they think they'll have better luck eating brains in Portland, Oregon.

Zombies don't start arguments on the internet about whether or not they are eating brains ironically.

They just fucking eat brains.

And maybe that's why we fantasize about killing them so much. The shambling bastards make us feel lazy.

Perhaps we should stop thinking about how successful we will be in slaughtering our reanimated friends and neighbors in the inevitable zombie apocalypse and spend more time with ourselves. Who do we want to *be* before the apocalypse comes?

What if we all focused on our own inner zombies? What if we pursued our life passions with the indomitable ferocity of a zombie who wants to eat brains?

What is your eating brains? Is it climbing a mountain? Playing the bassoon? Becoming fluent in modern conversational French? All of the above?

Set your sights on your goal and let your inner zombie go! Stumble-walk as fast as you can! Smash through the glass! Rattle the fence until it falls over! If someone chops your legs off with a heavily discounted wood axe from Walmart, then dig your fingers into the very ground and drag, drag, drag your chomping jaws to victory!

Because the only way to truly *emotionally* prepare for the zombie apocalypse is to lead a life that is worth fighting to keep.

When you have achieved this goal, you can happily look forward to the zombie apocalypse when you will be standing at the top of a mountain bashing brains with a bassoon and swearing at the undead in conversational French!

Your joyous screams will echo through the countryside: "Je te tue avec mon basson, tu baises zombie montagne!"

That is French for, "I kill you with my bassoon, you fucking mountain zombie!"

But until that happy day, all you can do is get out there in our pre-apocalypse world and chase down your dreams.

Now, go, my friends, go out there and eat the metaphorical hell out of some jerk's brains—like only you can.

GEEK TOPICS COVERED

▫ Zombies   ▫ The Apocalypse   ▫ *Highlander*   ▫ The Internet   ▫ Xbox
▫ Ordering Things from Amazon   ▫ Making Fun of Hipsters

4
ME LIKE TACOS

At Bizarro Taco Bell, all employees *must* wash their hands before using the bathroom.

GEEK TOPICS COVERED

❏ Bizarro Superman   ❏ Questionable Hygiene   ❏ Tacos

5

WORD PORN

This story was originally written for a friend of mine who loves two things: words and mythology. By words, I mean he loves big words that make him feel smart at the expense of others. And by mythology, I mean fantasy. And by fantasy, I mean cheap swords and sorcery fantasy like a combination of He-Man and softcore pornography. Actually, He-Man pretty much is softcore pornography, isn't it?

This is a fantasy story starring words. This is WORD PORN.

ONCE UPON A TIME IN THE LAND OF DICTIONARY, THERE LIVED A WORD called Indefatigable. Indefatigable was a huge leviathan of a word. His scandalously long vowels and hard consonants caused other words to swoon and sway. Their syllables would spread wide, revealing their trembling trochees and gliding diphthongs in an orgiastic fit of phonetic submission.

But there was only one word in the entire land of Dictionary that Indefatigable had eyes for: Pulchritude. Now there was a noun! Pulchritude's undulating flow, harsh rhythm, and wanton popping of her plosive P were almost unbearable. There was no adjective to describe Pulchritude with the exception of her sister, Pulchritudinous.

But all was not well in the land of Dictionary—a word of great evil was gathering power. A flabby, jaundiced, heinous word known only as Oleaginous.

Oleaginous had hatched an unspeakably odious plot to slaughter every word between himself and Pulchritude so she would be forced to live directly next to Oleaginous and endure his fetid polysyllabic advances.

Oleaginous, together with his lugubrious henchmen, Squamous and Feculent, marched through the lower O lands of Dictionary, murdering O word after O word with feckless disregard for their antiquity. They silenced Oration! They beheaded Overpass, defenestrated Overthrow, and ripped a gaping hole right through the center of Ozone.

Word of the atrocity traveled to our hero, Indefatigable. Together with his chatty sidekick, Loquacious, Indefatigable set off on a perilous venture to rescue his coveted noun.

As Indefatigable raced through the land of Dictionary, Loquacious babbled and chattered in a desperate attempt to provide comic relief that was neither humorous nor particularly successful in facilitating an emotional catharsis.

"Looky there," squawked Loquacious like a socially challenged eunuch, "Larceny is having a lark with Laxative!"

But Indefatigable could not be consoled. He raced forward, pausing only to wave a friendly hello to his good friends Libido, Liqueur, and Lubricant.

Meanwhile, the villainous triumvirate of Oleaginous, Squamous, and Feculent plundered a path through the hills, valleys, and streams of P. They perforated Penetration! They plastered Pedantic and sent Perdition straight to hell! They pricked Promiscuity and popped Prophylactic! Oleaginous was almost within propinquity of Pulchritude. All he had to do now was pass through Puberty.

Suddenly, Indefatigable burst upon the scene. Pulchritude told him to capitulate to Oleaginous as she was more than capable of defending herself. But Indefatigable was intransigent.

"You've killed a lot of good words today, Oleaginous," said Indefatigable. "And I'm going to make you pay."

The two big, hard to say words stared at each other with mutual loathing. Wind whistled atop the rocky plateau upon which they stood. Lightning slaked the dark clouds' hunger for illumination. And all the other words in the land of Dictionary gathered to witness this horrific conflagration.

Tension paced back and forth. Histrionic wailed and moaned. Ellipsis waited to see what WOULD... HAPPEN... NEXT...

Suddenly the titanic battle began! Swindle barely had time to collect bets before it was over. Without breaking a sweat, Indefatigable had ripped Oleaginous into his component parts leaving a hideous splatter of flaccid letters pooled in their own fluid. An alphabet soup of death.

The crowd began to disperse when Indefatigable cried out, "Oh, I'm not done yet!"

His tireless eyes met with the unfathomable beauty that was Pulchritude's pupils.

Even Loquacious was speechless as Pulchritude mounted Indefatigable like an umlaut on a U. They copulated for what seemed an incalculable time, an astounding epic of hammering, pounding, and punctuating, the two words riding one another like prurient asterisks.

It was too much for most decent words. Hell, it was too much for most naughty words. Fellatio's jaw fell open in shock. Sodomy turned his back. Even Fuck blushed.

Finally, in a swelling exclamation of teleological bliss, Indefatigable and Pulchritude climaxed, their syllables intertwined in an obscene mockery of a compound word.

And that, word lovers, is the true story of the invention of the word: In-pul-chrat-ah-ga-tude-able.

Or to describe this linguistic union in more pejorative terms: Their disgusting, spasmodic lovemaking had created a lovely new word that simply means "tireless beauty."

Because sometimes even ugly things can be pretty.

GEEK TOPICS COVERED

❏ Fantasy ❏ He-Man ❏ Annoying Sidekicks ❏ Big Words

6
A BRIEF TED TALK

Someday I hope to present a TED talk entitled *Kiss My Ass: Problematic Literalism in Contemporary Insults*.

GEEK TOPICS COVERED
❏ TED Talks   ❏ Hope

7

A DEATH STAR TO GUIDE ME

The following is a letter I wrote as a young boy in an alternate timeline. In this alternate timeline, Santa Claus receives this letter and I grow up to be all boring and well adjusted.

DEAR MR. CLAUS,

My name is Joseph Aaron Scrimshaw. The adults in my family call me Joey. I hate that. I tell them my name is Joseph. They laugh and call me cute. I tell them their reaction is condescending and pejorative. At this point, most adults leave the room.

Their loss.

But back to subject matter that is more germane to this missive. In regards to my Christmas present this year, it is my deepest desire to be the first child on my block to own a Death Star Space Station playset inspired by the major motion picture event *Star Wars*.

Now Santa, I realize you are probably not a fan of this recently released sci fi/fantasy epic since you are of the older generation and probably prefer more adult fare such as *Annie Hall*, *ABBA: The Movie*, or *Exorcist II: The Heretic*.

Suffice it to say, like yourself, *Star Wars* is rooted in ancient mythologies. Its timeless narrative allows young people to vicariously live a life of noble heroism through the main character, Luke Skywalker.

The film reminds us that we all have exciting destinies. As soon as a fascist regime brutally murders our parents or guardians, oh the adventures we will have!

At the end of the film (after his second parental figure, Obi-Wan Kenobi, has also been murdered) Luke Skywalker deals a terrible blow to the Galactic Empire by destroying the aforementioned space station, the Death Star.

The film's phenomenal box office success has generated an unprecedented wave of merchandise. There are *Star Wars* glasses, posters, cereals, pillowcases, ornaments, etc. In Germany, you can even get *Star Wars* toilet paper.

Wiping your ass with an image of C-3PO seems like an odd way to express your interest in the film. But then, it's Germany. I don't need to tell Kris Kringle how weird the Germans can be.

(As a side note: I am so completely surrounded by the œuvre of *Star Wars*, I often wonder if it will warp my mind and lead me to an adult life in which I obsessively quote the film and pretend any long cylindrical item I see is a lightsaber. So it goes.)

The most popular tie-in product is the Kenner toy company's line of action figures. Action figures are like dolls that don't threaten your masculinity. As much. The Death Star is a playset for these action figures. Sort of like Barbie's mansion, but evil.

And speaking of evil, I realize the irony of celebrating the birth of Jesus Christ by receiving something called the Death Star. I could argue that there is a STAR connection to the story of Jesus' birth, but I think we both know I would be equivocating.

I ask you to judge the Death Star not by the blatantly evil name (in fact, one wonders how the Empire got this name past the steering committee. Perhaps the Force was used?) or the inflated suggested retail price of $49.95, but rather judge it by the joy it would bring to me, young Joseph Aaron Scrimshaw, a sensitive young man trapped in the barren wastes of the frozen tundra that is northern Minnesota.

(Another side note: Northern Minnesota is much like the North Pole if most of the elves were alcoholics and Mrs. Claus had never heard of contraceptive devices. That is to say it is lacking in magic.)

Rest assured, Santa, that I have exhausted every other possibility for acquiring the Death Star. I have asked my extremely young hippie parents to buy it for me. They answered a firm "no," shaking their needlessly long hippie hair.

Even both of my grandmothers put together to form a sort of financial Mecha-Grandmother could not afford the

Death Star. I find this hard to believe as I have personally witnessed my maternal grandmother smoke at least $60 worth of Virginia Slims cigarettes in one sitting.

And so, Santa, as holographic Princess Leia said to Obi-Wan Kenobi, you are my only hope. I risk no hyperbole when I say my entire worldview for the rest of my life hangs in the balance.

I realize the Death Star is merely a collection of cheap plastic with orange foam used to clumsily symbolize the garbage in the trash compactor. However, what magic has been fused into the plastic? Is it really an overly priced commercial tie-in? Or is it like a star itself? Both a muse to sentimental poets and a very real giver of light, warmth, and life?

If I receive the Death Star, I will be justified in my current belief that the world is a bright and happy place in which one can always make one's dream a reality.

OR these fragile beliefs could be ruthlessly shattered by YOU. I will be sentenced to a long and hollow life devoid of joy, compassion, and love. I will spend my Death Star-less days constantly seeking out positive reinforcement by performing comedy shows in which I till the barren soil of my childhood in an attempt to amuse strangers in exchange for money.

Suddenly $49.95 doesn't sound that expensive, does it?

Yours with much affection, and admittedly no small amount of passive-aggressive guilt tactics as well as a healthy amount of skepticism about your existence (after all, my mother can only remind me that *Star Wars* isn't real so many times before I start questioning the reality of a morbidly obese elf who "can see me when I'm sleeping" and yet needs a letter to know my dreams), and, of course, love and admiration,

    Joseph Aaron Scrimshaw

    P.S. I must warn you in advance, I will not be able to leave any cookies out for you. As I mentioned earlier, my mother is a hippie. I hope you enjoy her seasonal collection of dried fruits and unsalted nuts.

    Merry Christmas and may the Force be with you... sometimes.

GEEK TOPICS COVERED

❒ *Star Wars*   ❒ The Death Star   ❒ Alternate Timelines   ❒ Mecha-Grandmother

8
THE SENSITIVE GENERATION

Every year, I celebrate the anniversary of the first broadcast of *Star Trek: The Next Generation* by avoiding conflict and talking about my feelings.

GEEK TOPICS COVERED
❏ *Star Trek*   ❏ Special Days   ❏ Special Feelings

9

FOR YOUR EXPENSE REPORT ONLY

The following is a handwritten letter that has been painstakingly transcribed. It reveals the shocking truth about wasteful government spending. After reading this you will be filled with rage at how much of our taxes are going to support the extravagant lifestyles of suave yet savagely violent super spies.

DEAR GOVERNMENT,

Just prior to my most recent mission, I was rebuked for not handing in more detailed expense reports.

Here is the expense report I handed in after OPERATION: MORNING THUNDER:

> I spent some money while risking my life to save our country from certain doom.

I received thousands of dead trees' worth of memos telling me that is not enough detail.

I had hoped to spare the building full of accountants the horror of the details. I am, after all, a hired killer whose mandate is to stop at nothing to achieve my goals.

I am also a civil servant and duty-bound to do every dumb little thing the government asks of me. So, at great personal risk, I constantly stopped what I was doing in the field to write every little thing down.

Included in this missive you will find a full account of my monetary activities for OPERATION: BUBBLE BLOOD BATH.

You will find that this document is splattered with red stuff. Much of it is blood. Some of it is tomato chutney. None of it is ketchup or catsup. I am not a savage.

There are other fluids, too. Bottom line, I would wear gloves to handle this. At least to handle it physically. I have nothing helpful to say about how you should handle it emotionally.

Sincerely,
Jack Thrust
Secret Super Spy

EXPENSE REPORT FOR OPERATION: BUBBLE BLOOD BATH

DATE	August 17
ITEM	A newspaper
COST	A few lousy cents

REASON FOR EXPENSE
My mission brief was printed in the newspaper. I had to sit at a wine bar and painstakingly decode it by tracking down the third letter of the second paragraph of every article in the lifestyle section.

DATE	August 17
ITEM	Three bottles of Château d'Yquem wine
COST	Less than $1200, which is a really good deal

REASON FOR EXPENSE
I was in a WINE bar doodling in a newspaper for five hours, I had to buy something.

DATE	August 17
ITEM	A notepad
COST	NOTHING.

REASON FOR EXPENSE
I realized I didn't have anything to write the mission brief down on (and I had been given strict instructions that this document was only for expenses), so I had to seduce a waitress and have sexual relations with her in the bathroom so I could surreptitiously remove her notebook from her apron.

CORRECTION
I guess I bought a condom from the bathroom vending machine. It cost fifty cents. It was purple and claimed to have grape flavor. My guess is that it just tasted purple. Is that enough detail for you?

MORE DETAILS
Here is the decoded mission brief written down on the notebook that only cost me a condom.

Your target is a rogue arms dealer from France code named Le Singe Mort. That is French for "Death Monkey." Le Singe Mort is believed to be undercover as a homeless person in New York City. He intends to sell a small Weapon of Some Level of Destruction to the highest bidder at a secret terrorist auction we believe he will hold in the sewers. (Side note from me: gross.) Your objectives are to secure the weapon, then capture or kill Le Singe Mort. (Side note from me: Just as a secondary objective, it would be really great if I didn't get captured and brutally tortured during this mission, unlike the last seven, but the fact that the government code named it OPERATION: BUBBLE BLOOD BATH doesn't exactly fill me with confidence.)

DATE	August 17
ITEM	About 32 cars
COST	More than most of the people reading this will make in their lifetime

REASON FOR EXPENSE

First let me say the three bottles of Château d'Yquem and the destroyed cars have no relation whatsoever.

After I left the wine bar, I got in a taxi to get to my hotel. Turns out the waitress I had inexpensive sex with in the bathroom of the wine bar was a spy who placed a tracker in my jacket pocket. Three black sedans filled with mercenaries began to follow my taxi and then opened fire on me with state-of-the-art laser-sighted machine guns. I returned fire from my government-issued revolver with the nine-bullet clip and mandatory silencer which diminishes accuracy.

Let me tell you, it's really good I had that silencer. I definitely felt like I was the person in the horrible gunfight who was breaking the least amount of noise ordinances.

Anyway, I managed to shoot out the tires of two of the black sedans causing them to flip, spin, roll, and just generally smash into every other car on the road. My apologies that I incurred some property damage while trying not to die.

The gunman in the third sedan successfully shot the driver of my taxi in the head, at which point I leapt out of the speeding taxi which proceeded to crash into the lower level of a parking garage. The taxi then exploded, causing several of the other cars in the parking garage to ignite and consequently explode.

In an effort to save my life and minimize taxpayer expenses, I disappeared in the crowd and walked the rest of the way to my hotel.

DATE	August 18
ITEM	A bottle of vodka and a DiGiorno frozen pizza
COST	Grossly overpriced

REASON FOR EXPENSE

What is the point of living if you can't feel alive?

CORRECTION:

Look, I don't want anyone to think I bought a lousy fucking frozen pizza on purpose. After I returned to the hotel, I wanted to distract myself from my near-death experience with some fine food and drink. I ordered an artisanal quattro formaggi pizza and a bottle of Grey Goose. I was delivered a DiGiorno cheese pizza and a bottle of White Eagle. I choked down the pizza and used the White Eagle vodka to try to get the bloodstains out of my tailored shirt.

DATE	August 18
ITEM	A high-class escort
COST	I actually made a profit

REASON FOR EXPENSE
After I ate the gross pizza and *attempted* to clean the blood out of my clothes, I just felt a little bummed out. I requested a high-class escort be sent to my room. When the escort arrived, she provided a wide selection of condoms which saved the taxpayers another expense. We then had sexual relations in a variety of positions in a variety of locations throughout the hotel room for the majority of the night. She enjoyed our carnal union and declined any payment. She even left me a tip.

DATE	August 19
ITEM	A city block
COST	How can you put a price tag on history?

REASON FOR EXPENSE
After getting only a few hours of sleep, I walked approximately three city blocks to the closest haberdashery to replace my blood-stained and vodka-soaked shirt. The haberdasher very promptly provided me with a new shirt. Just as I was about to try it on, several bullets pierced the shirt. Turns out, the high-class escort was also a spy who had given my location to Le Singe Mort's men who then followed me to the haberdashery.

Another gunfight ensued.

This disgusted me on an emotional level because having a gunfight in a fine men's outfitter is like taking the Lord's name in vain in a church.

Regardless, I did my duty.

I shot two of the six assailants splattering their blood on a number of fine tuxedos and causing one of them to crash into a display of cufflinks, no doubt scuffing them beyond repair.

At this point, one of the men took the haberdasher hostage. In an attempt to save his life, I laid down my weapon and surrendered, but not before discretely folding up the expense report and hiding it in my mouth. After all, I really wanted to focus on the most important things in that moment.

I was then taken to the basement of the haberdashery where I was bound and gagged with fine silk ties and beaten with wooden shoe horns for several hours. My manhood was then menaced with a knife that had been fashioned out of a wire hanger designed to display cummerbunds.

At this point, I nodded my agreement that I would "talk."

As the designer necktie was removed from my mouth, I used my tongue to place this very expense report between my teeth. I then lunged forward and attempted to administer paper cuts to my chief interrogator's eyeballs. I don't mean to brag, but it totally worked. I apologize for the fact that this super-important government document is covered in saliva and spurts of eyeball blood.

I then managed to strike several of my assailants with the legs of the chair injuring them and loosening my bonds.

Once I was free of the chair, I picked up one of the assailants' weapons and fired, I will admit, somewhat wildly. There were many screams of pain, fountains of blood, and some brain matter in the air. I stooped to retrieve the all important expense report from the floor. I then checked the body of one of the mercenaries for clues. I found a card with an address written on it. It was at this point I heard an ominous hissing sound coming from the heating equipment. I am very familiar with that sound. It is a sound that says, "Hey, don't mean to rush you, but there is going to be a gigantic fucking explosion any second now."

I raced up the stairs, pausing briefly to pick up the unconscious body of the haberdasher, and then ran outside.

Moments later, there was a massive explosion. Both the haberdasher and myself were thrown forward. I'm sorry to say my stolen gun also grazed a Porsche causing a minor ding. So I guess this expense item should have read, "A full city block and some detailing on a Porsche." Sorry.

DATE	August 18
ITEM	13 martinis
COST	Part of my soul

REASON FOR EXPENSE

Bloodied, bruised, and still in need of a new shirt, I returned to my hotel to regroup. Once in the safety of my room, I ordered a baker's dozen of gin martinis and drank them all.

After that, I started thinking pretty clearly. I pulled out a map of the city and located the address on the mercenaries' card. (Side note: When I was going through the pockets of the mercenary I noticed he was not carrying an expense report form. Just so you know.)

I made a plan to check out the address.

"FOR YOUR EXPENSE REPORT ONLY"

DATE	August 19
ITEM	A new suit
COST	Reasonable

REASON FOR EXPENSE
See previous, re: shooting, beating, torture, explosions

DATE	August 19
ITEM	Gourmet breakfast, brunch, lunch, afternoon snack, dinner, and late dinner
COST	Slightly less than a two-year technical college degree in computer animation

REASON FOR EXPENSE
If I'm going to die tomorrow, I'm not going to have the coroner finding frozen fucking pizza in my stomach.

DATE	August 19
ITEM	Two hours on a phone sex chat line
COST	Quite affordable for the first few minutes

REASON FOR EXPENSE
I was really tired of having sex with spies.

DATE	August 20
ITEM	A lot of stuff, but really the big ticket item is the Statue of Liberty
COST	I'm sure France will make us another one.

REASON FOR EXPENSE
Okay. This is NOT my fault.

Long story short:

I checked out the address. The house was empty but the basement floor had been jack-hammered open allowing access to the sewer.

I jumped down into the sewer immediately destroying my suit and my good mood. I followed a vagrant with a suspicious briefcase. This led me to the secret meeting set up by Le Singe Mort.

At the meeting, there was an array of terrorists from all countries including our own. On a table was a backpack with a big monkey on it. At the head of the table was Le Singe Mort himself. He sneered a lot and used big words. He didn't even use them correctly. So tired of "big words" villains.

Le Singe Mort revealed the monkey backpack contained a nuclear bomb. Frankly, I was kind of bummed out about this. I was hoping for something more bizarre like a radioactive monkey or a mood bomb that would make the world sad. You know, something exotic or romantic like the old days. But no, just another dime-a-dozen suitcase nuke stuffed in a backpack. Okay, a backpack with a monkey on it, but still.

The terrorists kept haggling about the price of the bomb.

I admit, I got bored. I pulled out my silenced pistol and killed as many of the terrorists as possible. During the exchange of gunfire, Le Singe Mort grabbed the nuke and ran.

I gave chase. Le Singe Mort exited the sewer and entered a nearby hospital. As I entered the hospital, I was incredibly dismayed to notice I had lost BOTH of my new cufflinks in the pursuit.

Le Singe Mort reached the roof of the hospital where he commandeered a helicopter. Not even a gyrocopter. A boring old helicopter.

As the helicopter took off, I leapt from the roof of the building and grabbed on to the landing skids. I heard something rip. It was either my vest or a muscle in my back. Maybe both. Then Le Singe Mort and I went through the whole helicopter battle dance.

He flew crazy to try to shake me off, I managed to get in the cabin, he tried to shoot me in the face but I forced his wrist down and he shot the controls.

We started weaving all over the sky and wrestling like two virgins trying to get it on in the backseat of a Ford Taurus.

Of course, he has to make the damn small talk. He starts spouting off about changing the face of the world, all the people that have ever been mean to him, his obsession with monkeys, and how we're both murderers.

And then, he goes there. He actually said THE THING.

He said, "You know, we're not that different, you and I, Mr. Thrust."

I kind of lost my temper and karate chopped him in the throat. There was a big crunch and then he died. I mean, I probably could have shot him but I wanted to give taxpayers that one bullet's worth of savings.

I quickly opened up the monkey backpack to make sure the nuke wasn't going to go off or anything.

There was no nuke. There was just a note that said, "Vainglorious dolts."

I bet Le Singe Mort didn't even know what "vainglorious" meant. He just wanted to use big words.

So I just kind of sat there for a second taking in the fact that I had been brutally beaten, many people had died, two suits had been ruined, and a decent amount of money had been spent to retrieve a monkey backpack with an immature note in it.

Then I looked up and saw that the helicopter was about to crash into the Statue of Liberty.

"FOR YOUR EXPENSE REPORT ONLY"

I tried to change course but the controls were useless. I was about to jump out of the helicopter, but then I stopped myself. First I double-checked that I still had the now massive wad of papers comprising this ALL-IMPORTANT EXPENSE REPORT.

Then I dived from the helicopter into the harbor as the helicopter kind of sort of exploded in the Statue of Liberty's face.

But on a positive note, I did survive. The government has spent a lot to train me, so I'm really glad I didn't put a dent in anyone's wallet by dying.

So, yeah.

Then I tried to check out of my hotel, but someone had blown it up because they thought I was still in there. So by all means, subtract my hotel bill from the total below.

TOTAL EXPENSE SUMMARY FOR OPERATION: BUBBLE BLOOD BATH
How many zeroes does a zillion actually have?

I hope this helps with your accounting. I'm going to go buy an enormous bottle of scotch and reflect on what it really means to be a secret super spy. I mean, what is this all about? Danger? Sex? Defending the concept of freedom? Saving the world? Saving the world ON A BUDGET?

Oh, that's right, it's about having a really tidy Excel spreadsheet.

—Jack Thrust

This is the end of
For Your Expense Report Only,
but Jack Thrust will return in
Death is a Reason to Live!

GEEK TOPICS COVERED

❏ Super Spies ❏ Awkward Relationships ❏ Frozen Pizza ❏ Guns
❏ Big Words ❏ Explosions ❏ Alcohol ❏ Adventure ❏ Explosive Alcohol Adventures

10
SO MUCH LUKE

My favorite *Star Wars* action figure is Bacta Tank Luke Skywalker because when you stop and think about it, you realize it's an action figure of Mark Hamill in a diaper.

GEEK TOPICS COVERED
❏ *Star Wars*   ❏ Action Figures   ❏ Nudity

COMEDY OF DOOM

11

THE THING THAT SHOULD NOT BE UNDER YOUR BED

My favorite horror author is H.P. Lovecraft. For any readers not familiar with Lovecraft, he was an effeminate xenophobic anglophile who wrote dense, morbid prose about terrible monsters, dead gods, and the ultimate futility of human existence. So I wanted to take some of those ideas and make them more accessible to children. Enjoy!

There is a monster under your bed. Right now. It is going to kill you. And there is nothing you can do about it.

COMEDY OF DOOM

It's a very strange looking monster. It has a big scaly head, a long slimy body covered in wings, tentacles, and thousands of beady little red eyes. The monster stands on two heathen goat legs. Finally, the monster has a big slobbering mouth—right where it's vagina should be. A vagina with teeth is called a vagina dentata. This is a term you will only learn if you go to college and get a useless liberal arts degree. Even if you do learn it, where are you going to use it? Job interviews? Cocktail parties? Tasteless comedy books?

But you don't have to worry about that. You're not going to college. Because you are going to die. Tonight.

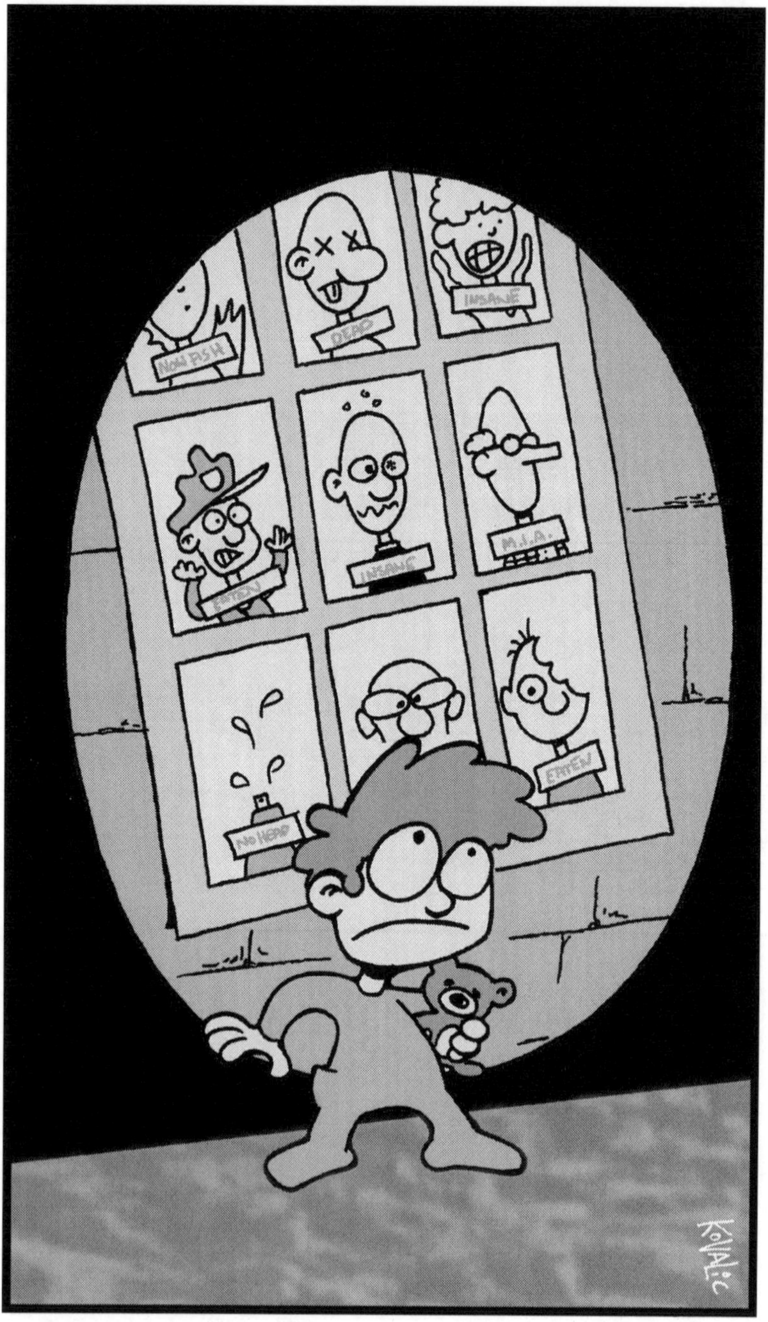
NOW FISH
DEAD
INSANE
EATEN
INSANE
M.I.A.
NO HEAD
EATEN
KOVALIC

Let's review some of the people in your neighborhood who can't help you. First, there's Mr. Policeman. If he doesn't immediately lose his mind just by looking at the monster, he might manage to fire off a couple of rounds from his tiny little gun. This is like casting a vote for a third-party candidate—it's a nice gesture but it's not really going to help anyone.

Then there's Mr. Priest. He's totally useless.

Now Mr. Librarian, he's your best chance. He has access to thousands and thousands of books filled with ideas and stories. Books are like chocolate you can eat with your mind. Unfortunately, some books aren't very good for you. For example, there's a book called *Ancient Socio-Cultural Iconography and Demonological Incantations for Dummies*. Also known as the *Necronomicon*. For some reason, Mr. Librarian is willing to check that book out to any yahoo with a library card and a photo ID. Which brings us back to your Daddy.

COMEDY OF DOOM

Your Daddy is actually the reason the monster is under your bed in the first place. You see, your Daddy is a cultist. Your Daddy used to think that people who dress up in weird robes, perform ancient rituals, and worship dead gods were bad people. Then he realized that was a pretty accurate description of most religions. "So," he reasoned, "what the hell?"

And before he knew it, he was out in the woods, buck naked, chanting in the obscene tongues of long-forgotten languages, and sacrificing innocent little bunny rabbits. One after another. Yep, your Daddy just couldn't kill enough cute bunnies. It was like Easter—an endless bloody Easter of death.

COMEDY OF DOOM

The end. I know, right? It seems sudden, but really what more is left to be said? There's a monster under your bed and it's going to kill you. We've known all the important information since page one, haven't we? And yet you would like a moral to give a sense of conclusion to the story, wouldn't you?

That's why we tell stories, isn't it? We flail and grasp at our lives and try to wrestle them down into something reasonable with a beginning, middle, and end when in reality, we have no control over most parts of our lives. Certainly not the beginning. Sometimes the end. But mostly we just get to fumble about with the middle. Fumble, fumble, fumble go the humans. And if in our fumbling, we happen to discover that narrative structure is nothing more than a fancy paint job designed to cover up the poor workmanship in the universe's construction, so what?

It's nice to share stories with friends. Stories that make us laugh and cry and think about different nice ways we might fumble around with the middle of our lives. Stories are fun.

Unfortunately, yours is over. Because there exists in this world a thing that by all human standards of decency should not be. And it's under your bed right now. So to all you other children out there who get to go on living: Good night, sleep tight, and don't let the vagina dentata bite.

GEEK TOPICS COVERED

❐ Horror   ❐ H.P. Lovecraft   ❐ Cultists   ❐ Librarians   ❐ The Horror of Reality
❐ The Intrinsic Fallacy of Narrative Structure   ❐ Bunnies

12
A PUBLIC SERVICE ANNOUNCEMENT

"Spleen" is a funny word. "Pants" is a funny word. "Spleen Pants" is a serious medical condition.

GEEK TOPICS COVERED
▫ Spleen   ▫ Pants   ▫ Medical Conditions

13
SUPER MARIO SUBTEXT

CHANCES ARE GOOD THAT IF YOU HAVE EVER PLAYED A VIDEO GAME, YOU have played *Super Mario Bros.* I myself played the game a lot in my youth. And by youth I mean sixth grade through right now. Seriously, it is very likely that as you read this, I am in a basement playing some version of *Super Mario Bros.*

For anyone unfamiliar with the basic story, our hero is an Italian plumber named Mario. He is dressed in bright red overalls, a red cap, and sports a big manly mustache. When he speaks, it's in brief high-pitched Italian exclamations such as, "Let's a-go!"

Mario also has a brother named Luigi. Luigi is basically the same as Mario except he wears green overalls, he's been put on a rack to be stretched out, and then repeatedly punched in the head so he always looks scared and a little drunk.

Mario and Luigi can be found doing many things such as golfing, go-kart racing, charting solar systems, and prescribing medication. The one thing you will never see them do is any fucking plumbing.

Mario also has a perky high-maintenance Southern belle girlfriend named Princess Peach Toadstool.

Here's the thing about Princess Peach: She's always portrayed as perfectly competent to kick anyone's ass.

She could rescue herself no problem but insists on making Mario do it. This is the video game equivalent of calling up your significant other at work and asking them to drive home and scratch your nose for you. Any sane person would ask, "Why? It's your nose. On your face."

And the only response from your partner would be, "And can you also bring your weird-ass brother?"

But I digress. Let's return to the days of my youth when *Super Mario Bros.* secretly embedded in my pubescent mind everything I would ever need to know about sex and sexuality.

Mario achieves his goals by being manly and aggressive. He jumps on things and hits almost everything he can find with his head: bricks, pipes, and even clouds.

Think about that. He is so manly, *he head-butts the sky.*

To be at the height of his powers, Mario has to consume various fungus and flora. Here is our first sexual safety lesson. Mario takes a mushroom to make himself larger. After this herbal supplement, your Mario becomes engorged and powerful. It's all very natural until you get cocky and pick up a flower with your bare hands. When you take the flower without protection it makes your large Mario burn.

Yes, you have the advantage of being able to shoot balls of fire from your hand, but at what cost?

If Mario wants to make a different choice, he can also get powers from a dancing star named Starman. When Mario jumps on top of Starman, he begins to sparkle and sing. It is obvious the game is reminding youthful players that there are alternatives to the heteronormative choices presented by less cosmopolitan video games such as *Pac-Man* or *Q*Bert*.

But the biggest lesson taught by the original *Super Mario Bros.* is the overall arc of sexual longing and expectation. To put it bluntly: Princess Peach is a cock tease.

You spend every waking moment striving to rescue her. Your Mario becomes large, then small again, then large again. You burn, you drown, you fall from incredible heights, you get hit by flying hammers, you swear so loud the neighbors knock on the door to ask you if someone is dying.

That's a, uh, true story.

At the time you think no one else could possibly be so deviant as you to imagine that, when you finally win the game, there might be a bonus level in which you consummate your quest with the grateful princess.

Then you get older and spend some time on the internet and realize you were not alone.

If you're like me, you start to really picture what this theoretical bonus level would actually look like.

Mario would go over to Princess Peach's castle with a bouquet of non-fire flowers. He would make some ravioli and open a nice bottle of pinot noir. Maybe Mario would fix her toilet since he is a fucking plumber. Then one thing would lead to another, Princess Peach would dim the lights, and Mario would put on some romantic music—something repetitive, penetrating, and totally 8-bit. Princess Peach's fluffy dress and Mario's bright overalls would fall to the floor.

Finally, the princess and the plumber would begin to copulate. You know exactly what this would look and sound like because you have been watching Mario bang things for the entire game. There would be a disturbing cartoon "boing" sound.

BOING! BOING! BOING!

And as always happens when Mario gets lucky, coins would be flying all over the place. Thousands of coins coming from God knows where!

COIN!

COIN!

COIN!

COIN!

1-UP MUSHROOM!

COIN!

And all the while, your creepy brother Luigi is lurking around the corner waiting to see if you die so he can get a chance to play.

All of this bonus level horror adds up to a few simple life lessons it took me a long time to decode.

1. Sex is not a reward. If you do a bunch of abusive stuff just to impress someone you're not a hero. You're a masochist.

2. Choose your partners carefully. There's a word for people like Princess Peach: crazy. Don't date crazy people. Mario is a Peach-enabler. Don't be a Peach-enabler.

3. If a young person wants to find true romance, a good way to do that is to stop playing video games just for a little while. Put down the controller, open the door to the real word, take a deep breath and say to yourself, "Let's a-go!"

GEEK TOPICS COVERED

❏ Video Games ❏ Super Mario Bros. ❏ Pac-Man ❏ Q*Bert ❏ Awkward Relationships

14
A LEGITIMATE SUPERHERO SUGGESTION

I would absolutely buy a comic book starring a superhero called The Crafter. She would swing through the dark city on ropes of yarn and fight evil with a crochet hook and knitting needle nunchuks.

GEEK TOPICS COVERED
❏ Superheroes ❏ Crafting ❏ Ninjas

15
A COMPLETE GUIDE TO COMPETITIVE HUGGING

IN THEORY, GEEKS SHOULD LOVE SPORTS.

Sports are strangely narrative. Every game tells a familiar story. It's like hearing an old myth with an exciting new twist.

There's a terrific amount of minutiae to endlessly debate. So many people on the internet are saying INCORRECT things about sports right now. Why aren't we out there pushing up our sports glasses with the protective headgear and correcting them?

The answer, in many cases, is simple: DODGEBALL.

If you never played dodgeball as a child, here's how the game works: Teachers, the adults who are supposed to be educating and caring for children, give the large, freakishly muscular kids big inflated balls. These strong, silent serial-killer types are then invited to throw the balls at other children.

Often, the other children are sensitive daydreamers. They are busy thinking about things like:

Why does Saturn have rings?

Could Superman use his heat vision to microwave a potato?

Is dog the root word for dogma? And if so, why?

Am I intelligent because of genetic traits or because I'm willing to work hard and apply myse–

Then they get hit in the face with a ball.

You know, for fun. For SPORT.

I believe many geeks of my generation missed out on the inherent thrill of sports because we were not introduced to the *idea* of them. We were basically told to put on shorts and run for our lives.

It's sort of like your dad saying, "Hey, *Star Wars* is really cool. Let me show you."

And then whipping out a lightsaber and cutting off your hand.

"Isn't that awesome? Now let's go collect the trading cards!"

These are, of course, gross generalizations and I have to believe things are slightly different for younger generations of geeks. They have been trained to be physically superior to old geeks by the constant playing of video games. Kids who grew up playing *Halo* or *Angry Birds* could easily remove the wings from a fly with a lawn dart at a distance of fifty feet.

There's also something alienating about the attitude around a lot of professional sports. Often they are permeated with aggression and a dangerous celebration of violence.

Just a reminder: The goal of boxing is to hit another person so hard they are unable to get up.

I think it's important to differentiate violence from competition. Humans seem to have a natural propensity toward both. I would argue that competition can and should be separated from violence.

Here's a handy guide:

Hitting people is a crime.

Cutting pieces of imaginary digital fruit in half with a sword on your smartphone is a healthy way to relieve stress.

I've struggled for a long time to invent a sport that geeks and indeed all people could embrace.

I wanted to craft a sport that is kind and emotive, but doesn't try to disavow our desire to BE BETTER THAN SOMEONE ELSE AT SOMETHING.

And so, my friends, here it is.

A complete guide to the thrilling sport called COMPETITIVE HUGGING.

Let's begin with the basics of what you need to host a game of Competitive Hugging in your very own home:

At least four people and a ball.

"Why a ball?" you ask.

The answer is simple. I'm both an optimist and a realist. I hope that this sport will become a huge international phenomenon. In order for that to happen there needs to be a ball. Other countries might be more sophisticated, but America simply will not tolerate a sport that does not have a ball.

We have made an exception with hockey and allowed the ball to be called a puck. Whenever we feel embarrassed that a puck is not called a ball, we just blame Canada.

There is also no ball in badminton. In badminton we hit something called a shuttlecock. But badminton (or weird tennis) is not exactly highly regarded. I believe there are two reasons for this. First, it is not violent enough. If the shuttlecock had a sharp point or the feathers were dipped in poison, it would garner more respect. Second, it's called a *shuttlecock*. This makes most Americans uncomfortable. Badminton might as well be played with a *rocketjohnson* or a *commuterwang*.

The bottom line is COMPETITIVE HUGGING CAN'T BE PLAYED WITHOUT A BALL.

More on the ball later.

Here are the basics on how to play Competitive Hugging.

First, appoint a Hugging Judge. This person's rulings are final. Questioning the decision of the Hugging Judge is like asking a cat why it likes to take naps. You will just be stared at like you're an idiot.

The Hugging Judge controls the proceedings and demands the attention of the crowd with a Control Horn. A Control Horn is like a whistle but gentle. For quick pick-up games of Competitive Hugging, any wind instrument will do. An oboe is best if you have one. A simple recorder will do in dire circumstances. A slide whistle will suffice if used judiciously.

Under no circumstances may a kazoo be used as a Control Horn. A Hugging Judge must command respect. Kazoos make you look stupid. In fact, the only time I ever use the antiquated insult "nincompoop" is when I see some idiot trying to assert his or her authority with a kazoo. A sense of humor or an enjoyment of shenanigans is valued, but pure unadulterated straight-up nincompoopery has no place in Competitive Hugging. Grow up, nincompoops.

The players in Competitive Hugging are called Emotion Warriors.

The Hugging Judge and Emotion Warriors must all wear jumpsuits.

In the future, when the sport is an integral part of the worldwide economy, the jumpsuits will be covered with advertising. Emotion Warriors will have numbers on their chests, Google on their back, Dairy Queen on their shoulders, and Coke on their ass. There's a lot of surface area to work with on a jumpsuit.

Before combat can begin, a large circle must be created on the floor. The circle is known as the Embracement Zone or, colloquially, the Hugging Arena. The circle can be drawn with chalk or constructed out of throw pillows. Feel free to be creative. In the future, the circle will be made of exciting promotional things like fire or a wall of cheeseburgers.

The shape MUST be a circle. No arcane symbols or interesting shapes like trapezoids. Sorry, Freemasons and geometry nerds, but the flowing energy of a circle is crucial to the proper functioning of the Embracement Zone.

The Hugging Judge, armed with the authority of a Control Horn, selects the first two Emotion Warriors to engage in combat.

At the first toot of the Control Horn, the Emotion Warriors enter the Embracement Zone.

First, the Emotion Warriors must stare at one another for a minimum of fifteen seconds. Awkward laughter is permitted from the Emotion Warriors, the spectators, and even the Hugging Judge. A controlled spirit of playfulness is acceptable.

At the second toot of the Control Horn, the Emotion Warriors begin circling one another and speaking loudly about their feelings. They DO NOT take turns. This is a raw spilling of emotion. At this point, Emotion Warriors should be like wild animals who have a lot to say about their day jobs and their relatives. The goal is to both open yourself emotionally and absorb the emotional state of your hugging adversary.

At the third toot of the Control Horn, Emotion Warriors must stop moving and speaking. The Emotion Warriors stand close together. They are face to face in the center of the Embracement Zone.

The time for the hugging is almost at hand.

The room is ALIVE WITH TENSION.

It is at this point that the ball comes into play.

The Discretion Orb or, colloquially, the crotchball, is inserted between the groins of the Emotion Warriors.

It is imperative to remember Competitive Hugging is not a sexy thing. The Discretion Orb guarantees that players and spectators can focus on the essential ingredients of the hug and not any distracting activity in the nether regions.

Plus, the game needs a ball and it's got to go somewhere.

At the fourth toot of the Control Horn, the hugging begins.

Before we get too deep into the hugging, let's examine what hugging isn't.

BOTH COMBATANTS MUST HUG. If only one person is hugging that is not, technically, a hug. That is a slow, creepy tackle.

There is no traveling while hugging. Combatants' feet must stay firmly planted on the ground. A hug that awkwardly shuffles about the room is called a junior prom.

It is also important to note that while there is almost no difference between professional **wrestling** and aggressively awkward **foreplay, neither have any place in Competitive Hugging.**

So, to review, hugging is NOT groping, dancing, wrestling, or even the ambiguous activity known as roughhousing. Besides that, go to town.

A quality hug is simply a beautiful embrace between two consenting adults with a ball jammed in their crotches.

While the hug is happening, the Hugging Judge and the audience are closely observing everything that is going on all up in that hug.

When completed, each Emotion Warrior's performance in the hug is judged on the following criteria:

1. Pressure: How tight was the hug? Was one arm limp compared to the other? Was there an awkward popping noise? Did the combatants work together to keep the Discretion Orb in place?

2. Duration: Was the hug too short? Too long? Did it have one of those false endings that are actually just a gathering of strength before the second bout of hugging? Did one combatant try to pull out of the hug prematurely? Did one combatant try to cling to the hug after it was clearly over?

3. Authenticity: Were either of the combatants faking it?

Was there genuine emotional warmth? Did it feel like the combatants were saying "I understand" with their arms?

4. Style: What individual flair did the combatants bring to their hug? Did they add a gentle sway? A back pat? A slight squeeze? Contented sighing? What did the combatants do to make the hug their own?

5. Creep Factor: An unfortunate risk of Competitive Hugging. Did hands wander? Did one of the combatants make a point of trying to smell the other's hair? While some tears of joy are fine, did either combatant start blubbering? Did the Discretion Orb become displaced and if so was it handled professionally?

6. Dismount: Finally, did the hug end gracefully? Did arms get tangled? Did hair get caught in the zipper of a jumpsuit? Did a combatant audibly say, "Christ, I'm glad that's over," or something awkward like that?

Once the hug is completed, the Hugging Judge blows a short celebratory toot on the Control Horn and the audience applauds. The audience may NOT hug the Emotion Warriors. Save it for the Embracement Zone.

The Hugging Judge then asks each Emotion Warrior about their feelings. This must be kept extremely short. When it comes to sports, Americans despise talking about feelings almost as much as they love balls.

During the interview, Emotion Warriors are tempted to say blithe, repetitive bullshit such as: "You know, I just went in there and I did the best hugging I could."

This is banal and it will betray you as an emotionally distant hugger. Also, do not say ANYTHING about God.

You are hugging people for SPORT, any sensible god is just happy that you are not punching one another.

The Hugging Judge then shares his preliminary findings. The Hugging Judge may ask for audience feedback if elements of the hug's quality are in question. The Hugging Judge also has the right to request a sample hug from the Emotion Warriors. This will allow the Hugging Judge to verify any suspicions such as, "I think this combatant might be a hair sniffer."

After combatant feedback, audience response, and Hugging Judge verification, an overall score is awarded to the hug itself. The hug is declared one of the following:

A Success Wrap: An indisputably high-quality hug.

A Middling Hold: A passable hug.

A Fail Lock: It is clear that some embrace took place but to call it a hug is an insult.

If the hug is deemed a Fail Lock, both Emotion Warriors are eliminated.

If the hug is declared a Success Wrap, both Emotion Warriors receive two points. If the hug is declared a Middling Hold, both Emotion Warriors receive one point.

After the points are awarded, one and ONLY one Emotion Warrior is rewarded an additional point and declared the winner of the hug. The losing Emotion Warrior is then asked to take a seat in the NO HUG ZONE.

This may seem harsh, but it is called *Competitive* Hugging.

The victor continues to the next round of hugging. Play proceeds until all Emotion Warriors have had an opportunity to hug.

People who obsess over sports love odd made-up terms like "bogey" and "hat trick" and "grand slam." If one Emotion Warrior successfully survives a trilogy of huggings without being eliminated, that is referred to as a "Wedge Antilles." If one Emotion Warrior survives the entire game without elimination, that is to say this combatant has hugged them all, that is referred to as a "Pikachu."

It is now time for the high stakes end game known as the SUDDEN DEATH HUG.

The two Emotion Warriors with the highest scores enter the Embracement Zone. If more than two Emotion Warriors are tied for the high score, then all Emotion Warriors with the equally high score enter the Hugging Arena.

At the aggressive double toot of the Control Horn, one final, epic hug is performed. The goal is to hug as long and honestly as possible. When the Hugging Judge sees an Emotion Warrior begin to falter in their emotional commitment to the hug, they are tagged with the Control Horn and removed from the Embracement Zone.

The last Emotion Warrior standing is declared the victor.

By definition, everyone else is a big fat loser.

In that decisive moment, all the passion, blood lust, millions of dollars' worth of illegal Competitive Hugging betting, as well as statistic-based Fantasy Hugging battles are resolved.

But in truth, our game is not over.

The final step of the smallest or largest game of Competitive Hugging is the CONSOLATION ROUND.

There is now no doubt that the victorious Emotion Warrior is the best hugger in the room. That person will now hug every single "loser."

That's right. Even if you lose, you win. Because you get a world-class, kick-ass hug.

No rules. No restrictions. Literally no holds barred. No Control Horn or crotchball. Just full-on freestyle hugging.

Then everyone orders a pizza and watches a romantic comedy or whatever seems appropriate in the moment.

That is Competitive Hugging. A sport that says, "I don't mean to be mean, but if push comes to shove, I think I could probably be nicer than you."

I hope to see Competitive Hugging become a hugely popular sport in my lifetime. I hope to take my children to a giant hugging stadium and say, "I wrote this down in a comedy book and now look what happened."

But for now, Competitive Hugging will mostly be played in homes or backrooms of bars or comedy clubs.

While I feel very strongly about the rules I've laid down, feel free to bend or alter them to fit your needs and circumstances.

However, do NOT simply throw out all the rules. If you just get a bunch of people together in a room to randomly hug each other with no structure it will be super awkward. It will be like an orgy where no one is even willing to go to first base. Weird and gross.

Be civilized, for fuck's sake. Keep in mind what this is all about: Turning a simple human gesture into a fun and engaging sport.

And if anything goes wrong in your game, if there's confusion or hard feelings, just hug it out, my friends, hug it out.

GEEK TOPICS COVERED

❏ Dodgeball ❏ Correcting People ❏ Myths ❏ *Star Wars*
❏ Collectible Trading Cards ❏ *Halo* ❏ *Angry Birds* ❏ *Fruit Ninja*
❏ Wedge Antilles ❏ *Pokémon* ❏ Hugs ❏ Love

16

A DIFFERENT PERSPECTIVE ON CAT PICTURES

You realize some cruel human photographer just stood there watching while that poor cat was hanging in there, right? Bastard.

GEEK TOPICS COVERED
- Cat Pictures

17

THE REAL-LIFE ADVENTURES OF MURDER MASTER 9000

JERRY WRITHED ON HIS COUCH, THE CRUMBS FROM ANCIENT FROZEN pizza meals crunching audibly under his rampant full-bodied undulation.

"No! No! You stupid motherfudging piece of plastic motherfudgery!" Jerry screamed. "I hit the motherfudging B button! Were you made in motherfudging America? Is that why you don't fudging work? You slow nonresponsive motherfudging fecal-thing!"

He was attempting to engage the controller of his video game system in a dialogue. Unfortunately, the controller was nonresponsive.

Jerry was having a hard time in life.

He worked in a bleak office. His title was Junior Assistant Manager to the Senior Manager of Junior Assistants. As far as Jerry could figure out, his job was pulled straight from a Kafka novel. The primary purpose of his job seemed to be pretending he knew what the purpose of his job was so he wouldn't get fired.

The previous evening, Jerry's girlfriend had broken up with him. She was of the opinion that Jerry wasn't marriage material. When Jerry tearfully asked why, she responded that he wasn't goal oriented.

Jerry thought this was ridiculous. He spent a huge amount of his time reaching goals in video games. He was one of the few people he knew who had reached 100% completion on all primary missions and side quests in the notoriously difficult video game *Quest for the Neverstone.* The company that produced the game had even sent him a paper certificate. Jerry framed it and hung it on the wall next to the diploma for his liberal arts degree in philosophy.

His girlfriend told him she was looking for a man like her father. "When my father was young he wanted to be a magician, but he gave it up to be a postal worker because it was the responsible thing to do," she told Jerry. "Would you give up video games to be a postal worker?"

Jerry made a face he couldn't control. It was a mixture of outrage, incredulity, and mockery. Jerry tried to say something, but all that came out was this sound:

"Pfffffft!"

In that second, his girlfriend immediately became his ex-girlfriend. She stormed out, slamming the door. His framed *Quest for the Neverstone* certificate crashed to the floor. His college diploma clung desperately to the wall as if to prove its worth.

So on this particular evening, Jerry just needed to relax.

"Oh! Fudge me! Fudge me hard, right in the ear!" Jerry screamed. "I'm going to shoot you in the fudging face! Then I'm going to wait for you to come back to life, light you on fire with an incendiary grenade, and shoot you in the fudging face while it's on fudging fire! "

Jerry was playing a game called *Screams of Death II: Unrealistic Warfare*.

When characters were shot, they screamed a lot but no blood came out, so the game was rated "E for Everyone." This meant people of all ages could play together online.

It was even possible to chat with other players online. Jerry was wearing an elaborate headset that made it look like he was manning phones at a telethon or recovering from a massive neck injury so he could chat with his current opponent, a merciless fifteen-year-old girl with the screen name LadyKillKill.

"Ahh! You shot me in the face again!" Jerry said, reporting exactly what had just happened as video game players so often do. "I don't even have a gun right now and you shot me in the motherfudging crockpotting face!"

Jerry was using words like "motherfudging" and "crockpotting" because swearing wasn't allowed in Chat Mode.

Of course, everyone knew what "crockpotting" meant which often made Jerry wonder what was the fudging point in using a different word if the meaning was already culturally agreed upon?

But Jerry wasn't here to think. He was here to kill this motherfudging fifteen-year-old girl.

"Will you please, please for the love of fudge, stop shooting me until I can find a motherfudging gun, you merciless little shank-a-doodle!"

Jerry was just making words up now.

Onscreen, his avatar ran wildly about the post-apocalyptic urban hellhole world of the game. Above his character's head floated his online moniker, MurderMaster9000. The name was also accompanied by his ranking among online players. Jerry was ranked Death Bait. This was a colorful term to indicate Jerry was, in fact, more a master of being murdered than a master of committing murder.

"A gun! I see a gun! I'm going for it," Jerry strategized out loud.

He slammed his thumb into his joystick and his avatar rocketed down a dark corridor toward a small pistol on the ground.

Just as MurderMaster9000 was about to reach the gun, LadyKillKill popped out of the shadows and filled his screen. Jerry was blocked from reaching the gun.

"NOOOOOOOOOOO!" Jerry screeched as though getting this fake gun was the most important thing in his real life. "Please, *please*, just let me pick up the gun."

The vexingly casual voice of LadyKillKill pumped out of Jerry's headset. "I don't know. Why don't you get on your knees and ask?"

"There's no button for getting on your knees."

"You can crouch," chirped LadyKillKill. "Why don't you crouch? I just want you to be lower than me."

Jerry thought this wasn't possible on an emotional level, but he conceded. He depressed his secondary joystick and MurderMaster9000 squatted.

"All right, I'm squatting. Can I please waddle over and pick up the fudging gun now?"

"No."

"What more do you want from me?"

There was a long pause.

"I guess… I guess I was kind of wondering… Why do you even play this game?"

"Because," Jerry responded without hesitation, "it's fun."

"Really? You're squatting on the floor and you don't even have a gun."

"It's fun when I have a gun, all right?"

"I'm sure it's *more* fun for you then, but... But I mean on a deeper level, like, philosophically, why do you want to run around shooting people who are way super-younger than you? What's the point?"

"It's escapism, okay?"

"Really? 'Cause I'm holding you hostage right now. That's sort of the opposite of escape."

Jerry's face contorted and he growled, "Look, life is hard when you're an adult. Like really *fudging* difficult. It's all this work and responsibility and you have all these hopes and expectations you have to manage and you spend most of your time just scraping to get by and every time you start to get just a little bit ahead some crockpotter comes along and fudges the whole thing up! Does that make sense? On a *philosophical* level?"

Jerry pounded his controller on the couch for emphasis. His college diploma fell from the wall.

"Okay," said LadyKillKill. "I get that, but that doesn't sound that different from what happens to you when you play this game."

"I just want to shoot people, okay? I want to shoot people in the face. I can't shoot people in the face in real life!"

"Well, you can't shoot people in the game either. Your aim is terrible."

Jerry thrashed in frustration and the cord attached to his headset yanked his head painfully. "Arrgh! Why? Why are you doing this to me?"

"You mean holding you hostage in the imaginary game world or asking you to justify your life choices?"

"Both! Either! I don't know! I just want to accomplish something today. Is that okay with you?"

"Why don't you go do the dishes or clean your gross old-man bathroom or—"

"I don't want to do real-life things!" Jerry ranted. "I just... I just want to be someone else for a little while. Is that such a bad thing?"

"According to all the motivational posters hanging up around my high school, yes." LadyKillKill said brightly. "You should be happy being you."

Jerry settled firmly into the ass groove his frequent video-game playing had formed on the couch. He grasped the controller tightly. "Well, I'm not me, right now! I'm MurderMaster9000, dammit, and I'm about to do some murdering on your ass!"

And with that, Jerry's avatar suddenly popped out of Crouch Mode and began darting and weaving toward the little pistol.

What followed was a spastic ballet of age-appropriate violence.

MurderMaster9000 spiraled and pirouetted as LadyKill-Kill unloaded her clip, shooting him in the knee, the groin, the elbow. Jerry and his avatar screamed and screamed.

"AAAAHHH!" screamed Jerry.

"AAAAHHH!" screamed MurderMaster9000.

LadyKillKill ran out of ammo and quickly switched to the ludicrous Witch Slap Mode. Her hand lashed out and repeatedly smacked MurderMaster9000. His head jutted and recoiled at sickening but bloodless angles.

"Shinola!" said Lady KillKill as MurderMaster9000 finally reached his destination.

There was a tinny sound effect of a gun loading to indicate MurderMaster9000 had picked up the pistol.

Without getting up, Jerry performed an undignified victory dance. Any casual observer would think he was trying to give the couch a lap dance. "Ha! I have a gun! I have a gun! And you're stuck in Witch Slap Mode!"

Jerry hadn't felt this happy in days. There he, MurderMaster9000, stood with a fully loaded PP-3, the smallest, least deadly gun in all of *Screams of Death II: Unrealistic Warfare*. But in that moment the size of the victory didn't matter.

He had a gun. A stupid little gun. He had the basic means necessary to even play the game. He had made the smallest possible accomplishment.

It made him want to play the game for the entire rest of his life.

"You know, LadyKillKill, I could shoot you in the face right now," Jerry said, his crosshair dancing about LadyKillKill's forehead. Jerry's fingers trembled to get the perfect aim. "But maybe I should spare you, to show you how much better I am than you."

"Oh, just shoot me," LadyKillKill said with a smile in her voice. "I'll respawn in two seconds, kill you eight times, and level up for all the extra vengeance killing points."

Jerry tried out a tough-guy voice. "Oh yeah? *Bring it.*"

The cheap plastic controller danced in Jerry's sweating hands. His brain told his twitching, aching forefinger to squeeze the trigger button and as the command raced through his nervous system, his television suddenly froze and a text box popped on his screen:

> Dear MurderMaster9000: Our records indicate you recently used the words "dammit" and "ass" while in Chat Mode. You are suspended from online play for the next 72 hours and will be disconnected immediately.

Jerry heard something over his headset. Was it the connection going dead or the sound of LadyKillKill trying desperately to slap his avatar one more time before it disappeared?

"Son of a cocksucking motherfucking goddammit," Jerry whispered softly, almost peacefully.

He looked around at his filthy apartment.

He peeled his cramped fingers off the controller, picked up the remote, and turned off the television.

With some effort, he struggled up out of the comfortable grasp of the couch's ass groove and walked over to his diploma. Jerry picked it up and put it on the table next to his *Quest for the Neverstone* certificate.

He walked into the bathroom and stared at himself in the mirror. He looked pale and clammy like a drug addict. Or was the mirror just that dirty? How long had it been since he cleaned it?

Jerry reached under the sink and pulled out a large bottle of window cleaner with a trigger right under the spout.

He looked at himself holding his cleaning weapon. He tried out a few action poses. He was nowhere near as embarrassed as he felt he probably should be.

Then he took very careful aim at the reflection of his forehead. Jerry smiled, knowing he was at the very least going to get something productive done that night.

He spoke in a deep, gravelly voice. "All right, life. *Bring it.*"

Then Jerry squeezed the motherfudging trigger.

GEEK TOPICS COVERED

❏ Video Games   ❏ Online Gaming   ❏ Frozen Pizza   ❏ Couch's Ass Groove   ❏ Fantasy

18

A TERRIBLE BAT-EPIPHANY

Batman dresses up like a bat to strike terror in the hearts of criminals, right? But he's a ninja who can pop out of the darkness and beat the crap out of just about anyone. That's plenty scary all by itself. So he doesn't really need to dress up as a bat. Bruce Wayne is just… he's just… it's LARPing.

GEEK TOPICS COVERED
❏ Batman ❏ Ninjas ❏ LARPing

19

SENSE AND SEVEN MINUTES IN HEAVEN

One Valentine's Day I was poking around the internet and found something shocking: an unpublished Jane Austen erotica story called *Sense and Seven Minutes in Heaven*. Really, this was not written by me. It was written by Jane Austen. Which is odd, because there are a ton of f-bombs. Enjoy.

MINUTE ONE

IT IS A TRUTH UNIVERSALLY ACKNOWLEDGED THAT A SINGLE MAN locked in a closet with a single woman must attempt to engage in premarital fornication. However little known the feelings or views of such a man on first entering the closet, this truth is so well fixed in the minds of single women, that should the suggestion of wanton ribaldry not be made, a single woman is disposed to consider it an insult.

These truths were not lost on Miss Margaret Lucy Anne Cockingwood of Cockton Manor on Old Cockingham Lane nestled in the quaint village of East Poppingcockshire.

Maggie, as she was known to her closest friends, was

currently locked in a rather small closet with a legendarily dour gentleman named Mr. Frith Banbury Fannycock Cardington.

Mr. Cardington had protested greatly when the spinning bottle of port came to a definitive stop while clearly pointing in his direction with all the firmness and rigidity of a scolding dowager's jutting digit.

"I am ever so afraid, I must decline," whined Mr. Cardington. "I do suffer from allergies so."

But Maggie and the other dinner party guests had forced him into the closet as he bleated like a sheep about the dire risk of an apocalyptic sneezing fit.

And so Maggie and Mr. Cardington stared at one another's dimly lit silhouettes as the precious seconds ticked away and Mr. Cardington fumbled about for something interesting to say.

"I say," he said redundantly. "This small, tight space is rather damp, isn't it?"

"Not yet," responded Maggie with an equal mixture of annoyance and lascivious intent.

MINUTE TWO

MR. CARDINGTON WAS BAFFLED BY THIS BLATANT INNUENDO. "I'm sorry," he murmured, "come again?"

"At this rate, there shan't be time for that," grumbled Maggie.

"What?" retorted Mr. Cardington as though he hadn't just been bashed about the head with a rather obvious reference to multiple orgasms.

"Honestly, Mr. Cardington," Maggie huffed, "have you no sense of social decorum? We are in this closet for a most singular purpose. Do you know what it is?"

"No!" Mr. Cardington whisper-yelled.

"There are no end of euphemisms for it," Maggie protested. "Roasting the beef. Ringing for the butler. Braiding the wick. Visiting the stable. Polishing the soup spoon. It works with virtually any verb and noun, for heaven's sake!"

Mr. Cardington's ignorance was palpable. Indeed his confusion was as large as the British Empire itself, but ironically it appeared as though the sun would never rise on it.

"Mr. Cardington," Maggie blurted, "I simply wish to fuck you!"

MINUTE THREE

SADLY FOR MAGGIE, THE ONLY PART OF MR. CARDINGTON THAT stiffened was his upper lip.

"Miss Cockingwood," he lectured, "as a gentleman, I'm afraid that I cannot bring myself to even mention aloud, much less agree to, such an illicit act."

Maggie took a deep breath and launched into a lengthy speech about pride and pagan rituals and the hubris of British culture daring to impede the basic carnal knowledge to which flesh is heir, about sense and bisexuality, and the hideous damage sexual repression can do to the psyche of a nation. However, the thesis of her strident and eloquent argument could have easily been communicated with this compelling universal truth:

There is nothing sadder than a single man who will not put out.

MINUTE FOUR

THE NEXT THIRTY SECONDS PASSED IN SILENCE.

Time dragged forward with all the speed and warmth of a melting iceberg.

Finally, Mr. Cardington's defiant posture slumped in defeat as he mumbled, "Oh, bugger me, fine."

"We shall have to make haste," Maggie admonished. "We only have three minutes left."

Mr. Cardington cocked his left eyebrow and said, "That shan't be a problem."

Maggie kissed him furiously and the unlikely couple tore at one another's clothing with the elegance and precision of a drunk man carving a Christmas goose. It was as hideous as it was exciting.

MINUTE FIVE

THEY FUCKED.

MINUTE SIX

THEY CONTINUED FUCKING. THE SUDDEN LOVERS STUMBLED AND wrestled, kicking up dust, causing Mr. Cardington to sneeze repeatedly. The closet became a symphony of bizarre human sounds.

Sneezing, moaning, copulating, perhaps flatulating?

Who could tell?

And who cared?

What with all the fucking.

MINUTE SEVEN

STILL FUCKING!

Maggie reached for Mr. Cardington's fob. It was not a euphemism.

She reached into his waistcoat and popped open the watch. She was able to make out the time as Mr. Cardington's naked white ass was so bright it actually gave off a glow—a dim romantic light like a big, tight kerosene lamp.

"We're almost of time," Maggie moaned.

Mr. Cardington, ever the gentlemen, informed Miss Cockingwood he was simply waiting for her.

There was a polite round of offers from both parties to allow the other to climax first.

Mr. Cardington stated rather firmly that he would hear nothing of it. He argued that he had already violated his own sense of gentlemanly conduct by agreeing to fuck Miss Cockingwood in the first place and should he allow himself to climax prematurely he feared he would not be able to live with the shame.

What would they say in London?

Maggie began to rebuke Mr. Cardington for his baroque attitude towards orgasm etiquette when fate intervened.

At the exact same moment, five things happened.

Maggie climaxed.

Mr. Cardington climaxed.

The closet door fell open.

Mr. Cardington sneezed.

The rest of the dinner party guests stared in shock.

Luckily, they were all quite high on opium. They were also blinded by the sudden brightness of Mr. Cardington's luminous white ass, so no one was precisely sure of what they saw that night.

Later, Maggie and Mr. Cardington would agree that three out of the seven minutes they spent in that tight, damp closet in Cockton Manor on Old Cockingham Lane nestled in the quaint village of East Poppingcockshire were, indeed, heaven.

THE END.

GEEK TOPICS COVERED

❏ Jane Austen ❏ FanFic ❏ Rule 34 ❏ Allergies

20
THE DOOM FROM THE '70s

I wish Sid and Marty Krofft had produced an LSD-infused puppet show called *H.P. Love N' Craft*.

GEEK TOPICS COVERED
❏ The Kroffts   ❏ Puppets   ❏ H.P. Lovecraft

21

THE WRATH OF HUMANITY

WHEN I WAS A TEEN, A GIRL I LIKED CAME OVER TO MY HOUSE BECAUSE we had a social studies project together. I had an original series *Star Trek* poster hanging on my bedroom wall. The girl looked shocked and concerned by it.

"You should really take that down if you want, you know, stuff to happen in this room," she said. I laughed awkwardly. We did some social studies stuff together. Sadly, that is not code for anything sexy. She left. I looked at the poster. "Captain Kirk wouldn't take a poster of himself off his bedroom wall," I thought. "And he does fine with women. Screw it."

Now I'm friends with the girl on Facebook. She has a husband, three kids, some cats, and a dog. Sometimes she chats with my wife about knitting. She posted that she was enjoying watching old episodes of her favorite TV show, *Star Trek*.

Oh, the humanity.

If only *Star Trek* technology were real, I could slingshot my spaceship around the sun and go back in time. I could burst into my bedroom and old me would start ranting to young me about this thing called The Facebook.

"Everyone you know is on it! It's like a living museum of your entire life! People will post about TV shows they like! And you can hit a little button on your smartphone to let them know you like that they like that! The girl you like is going to like *Star Trek* in the future! She might even like it now! She could be lying to you!"

Young me would most likely respond, "Uh, what the hell is a smartphone?"

Old me would explain that it's a little computer you can hold in your hand. "It's like a tricorder except instead of analyzing people's heartbeats and the atmospheres of strange new worlds, it tells you the closest place to get a burrito."

Young me would stare off into space imagining this. "Can you talk to a smartphone?"

"Yes."

"Can it talk back?"

"Yes."

"Can you make it blow up by being irrational?"

Old me would stare off into space imagining this. "Uh, no. Sort of the opposite actually."

"What the hell does that mean?" young, inquisitive, prone-to-swearing me would ask.

"Look, *Star Trek* gets a lot of things right about technology, but the trope where Kirk can make computers blow up by talking bullshit doesn't really make sense in our world. We don't want computers to be aggressively logical, we want them to be intuitive and friendly and, well, human."

"How's that working out for humanity?" young me would ask with obnoxious teenage know-it-all sarcasm.

"It's fine," old me would say defensively. "Here, let me show you."

Old me would whip out his smartphone and demonstrate.

"Phone! In which episodes of the classic *Star Trek* series did Kirk blow up a computer by talking nonsense?"

The phone would answer, "There are no shops nearby that sell nonsense blowers."

"Phone! Look up index of *Star Trek* episodes!"

"Did you say *Star Trek* Windex?"

"Phone! For the love of Christ, listen to me!"

"There are several stores nearby that sell love."

"Okay, smartass phone, what is love?"

"Did you say watch love? You asked me to block all websites where you can watch love."

"Phone! What is love?"

"Would you like me to play a song by Dean Martin?"

"Oh, fuck off," old me would say and I would stuff the smartphone back in my pocket while "That's Amore" played gently in my pants.

Young me would stare at old me and then start pedantically rattling off the names of the episodes in which Kirk destroys computers with nonsense, "Um, 'The Changeling,' 'I, Mudd,' 'The Return of the Archons,' 'The Ultimate Com—'"

"Okay!" old me would interrupt. "Good for you! You still have the ability to remember things with your own human brain instead of looking them up on a computer all the time. Maybe you shouldn't be so damn proud that you can list the episode titles of original series *Star Trek* based on plot points."

Young me would bristle and say, "What the hell are you even doing here?"

"I came here to tell you that you shouldn't feel bad about liking *Star Trek* because in the future a lot of people are going to like it. Even the girls you like will like *Star Trek*. So just, you know, don't take your *Star Trek* poster down because of what that girl said."

"Okay," young me would say. "I wasn't going to take the poster down."

"Okay," old me would say.

"So," young me would continue, "you used what I assume is really amazing technology to travel back in time to show me that in the future human beings have successfully made tricoders that are capable of being just as moody, dickish, and ineffective as normal human beings?"

"Yes and no," old me would say. "I guess... I guess I just came here because I know that thing the girl said about *Star Trek* is really going to lodge itself in your brain. And things get fuzzier as you get older. You think you'll remember everything but you won't. You get so used to being able to look up any little fact you want about *Star Trek* on a computer, you forget you can't look up your own memories. There is so much you forget. But for some reason, that quote, that brief interaction is something you *remember*. And then, years later, you will see her Facebook status update about liking *Star Trek* and you will just stare in shock. You'll be like a big dumb old-timey super computer. Steam will come out of your ears and you'll mumble to yourself, 'Must not... can not... does not compute.' You will briefly consider responding, 'Hey, you told me you didn't like *Star Trek*. What gives?' But you will realize that is absurd because there is no way she is going to remember saying that to you. You sit there and wonder about all the thousands of offhand comments you've made that might be lodged in someone else's brain. You shake your head and go on with your day, because what the hell else are you going to do about it? You know?"

Then we would stare at one another. We would both feel a little bad about being such short-tempered smart-asses. We would look at the *Star Trek* poster on the wall and then back at each other. It would be very weird that through the mists of time and the changes in technology, we basically behave the same.

"So," young me asks, "do I still have the poster?"

Old me would think. "I don't know."

"What happened to it?"

"I don't remember."

We would both laugh awkwardly and old me would feel a great temptation to warn young me that *Star Trek V: The Final Frontier* wasn't going to be a very good film. Then old me would use his smartphone to beam out of there.

I would return to the present and check Facebook to see if that girl I used to like has anything new to say about *Star Trek*. Nope. She's really proud of her son for getting a good grade in algebra and she's pissed off that a rabbit ate her tulips.

I would get out my smartphone and look up which episodes of the original series feature Kirk blowing up computers with all his human bullshit.

I would start to watch one of the episodes instantly over the internet. I would realize I was being selfish. I would set the episode to play back from the beginning and wait for my wife to come home so we could watch *Star Trek* together.

Then I would sit in the dark, wondering if even-older me would travel back in time to tell me something else I already knew.

GEEK TOPICS COVERED

▢ *Star Trek*   ▢ Time Travel   ▢ Smartphones   ▢ Blowing Things Up
▢ Social Media   ▢ Awkward Relationships   ▢ Love

22

THE IDES OF MARCH

Every March 15, I'm disturbed to see that people are losing the spirit of the Ides of March. It's not just about stabbing. It's about coming together to stab in groups.

GEEK TOPICS COVERED
❑ Special Days   ❑ Stabbing

23

A SONG OF RAINBOWS AND ALSO RAINBOWS

Like many sensitive geeky types, I'm a big fan of the Muppets. When I was a wee small child desperate for *Star Wars* content, I was thrilled to see Luke Skywalker on *The Muppet Show*, even though I understood the appearance was non-canonical. I enjoyed all the Luke parts but I was frightened and confused by the song-and-dance number. Then I grew up, started doing theater, and learned the true meaning of fear and confusion. I started to appreciate the Muppets on a different level. As a kid, my favorite character had been Animal, a loud, disrespectful agent of chaos. As an adult, I feel terrible for Kermit. He's just trying to put on a show. Why can't the other Muppets put away their egos and chickens and explosives and sexual longing for twenty-two fucking minutes? More than anything I feel sorry that people are always giving Kermit shit about "The Rainbow Connection." I understand the line "Why are there so many songs about rainbows?" is stupid because there aren't really that many songs about rainbows, but come on, guys. Kermit has a lot on his plate. In an effort to help him out, I've written a song about rainbows. It's just the lyrics. Feel free to set it to any melody you want although I would suggest a mid-tempo rock ballad style. Now can we please just step off Kermit's tip?

First verse
You go out after a storm
Up in the sky, something forms
Just what is it? What's up there?
Is that a strand of clown hair?
Oh no, it's something better
Like the sky is wearing a sweater

Chorus
Rainbow, rainbow
You are made from rain
And also probably light
What is it about rainbows
that makes them so damn nice?

Second verse
Rainbows have so much to give
They show us Mister Roy G. Biv
They're so subtle yet so bold
How to describe what we behold?
Well here is a good place to start
Rainbows are science making out with art

Chorus
Rainbow, rainbow
You are made from rain
And also probably light
Double rainbow, double rainbow
You are the same thing
Only you are done twice
What is it about rainbows
that makes them so damn nice?

Guitar/flute/interpretive dance solo

Chorus
Rainbow, rainbow
You are made from rain
And also probably light
Double rainbow, double rainbow
You are the same thing
Only you are done twice
Triple rainbow, triple rainbow
The world can't cope with you
We would die; we would be through
Rainbow, rainbow, rainbow
Rainbow, rainbow, rainbow
Rainbow

Another solo if your lead guitarist/flautist/interpretive dancer has a big ego. Close with one last:

RAINBOW!

Okay. Maybe there is a reason people don't write more songs about rainbows.

GEEK TOPICS COVERED

❐ The Muppets   ❐ *Star Wars*   ❐ Double Rainbow   ❐ Science   ❐ Horror

24
THINKING OUTSIDE THE BRAIN

"There is a lot of meat in team."

—*Zombie motivational saying*

GEEK TOPICS COVERED
❏ Zombies ❏ Brains ❏ Eating ❏ Teamwork

25

CURSE OF THE NAKED MIME

"A mime is a terrible thing to draw in live nude model art class."
—Abraham Lincoln

OKAY, LINCOLN PROBABLY DIDN'T SAY THAT, BUT IF HE EVER HAD TO draw a nude mime in art class he sure as hell would have agreed with me.

One of my earliest memories is watching reruns of the 1960s *Batman* television show and drawing pictures of Robin the Boy Wonder. The pictures looked like this:

125

Little did I know that by drawing Robin the Boy Wonder I would set myself on an inevitable course to be stuck in a room with thirty other people staring at a mime.

A naked mime.

And what made it even worse—and who knew it could get worse—was the fact that this naked mime had the largest scrotum I have ever seen.

For a straight man, I've seen a lot of scrotums. I've done a lot of work in theater. In the fast-paced world of drama, with quick costume changes and small dressing rooms, scrotums abound. Anyway, this mime scrotum was freakishly huge.

The thirty people in the room involuntarily leaned forward—pulled in by the power of this mega-scrotum. Perhaps, however, we were all just straining to see his tiny, tiny penis.

Because for some reason if you have giant balls, you're going to get a wee tiny penis. That's just the balance of nature.

But back to Robin.

I remember my mother looking at the picture and saying, "Wow, you can draw well just like your dad and your brother." It was true. Scrimshaw men are naturally good artists with weird hair and tiny bladders. Again, the balance of nature.

I kept on drawing as I grew up.

When junior high rolled around, I discovered I could

get the attention of young girls by drawing cool pictures. I drew sensitive pictures of hands holding roses, I drew mean pictures of the members of New Kids on the Block being lit on fire by the members of Guns N' Roses. When things didn't work out with the young girls I was trying to impress, I would draw pictures of sad men in the margins of my homework. One of my teachers even called me on it. She announced in front of the class, "Um, Joseph, I took a few points off your book review of *War of the Worlds* because the crying man was making me sad."

Here's what the crying man probably looked like:

Hungry for even more junior high attention, I volunteered to work on the school play. It was a production of *Oliver Twist* set in apartheid-era South Africa. I got to play the beggar who said, "Please, sir, may I have some more?"

It was my first theatrical role. I was also asked to help paint the backdrops. There was one small problem. The junior high had borrowed backdrops from some grade school's production of *Oliver Twist*. Several of the backdrops featured portraits of the characters and their families. The portraits were all of white people. The cast of our play was mostly African-American. So the teacher in charge said, "Hey, Scrimshaw, you can draw, right? Can you paint these white portraits up to look black? Thanks!"

I made a desperate bumbling attempt to paint an African-American skin tone over the white portraits, but I missed spaces near the eyes and lips so when you stepped back it looked like the set was covered with horrible portraits of Al Jolson.

Here is a space in which I refuse to show you a drawing of what that looked like:

I begged one of my friends who was a better artist than me and actually, you know, African-American to help me fix it. She did and my reputation as an artist was saved.

I continued to draw and paint throughout high school. I knew I wanted a degree in visual art, but I wasn't sure where I wanted to go. Eventually, something drew me to the University of Minnesota. Turns out, it was the gravitational pull of the naked mime's scrotum.

The first day of my first drawing class at the University of Minnesota started with a lecture about respect. We were all freshman and we were all going to be in the same room with live nude models.

Awesome. I was really anxious to work on drawing the live human form. And if one of the models happened to be an attractive young lady, well, that was a fringe benefit I could quietly and respectfully enjoy.

The next day, we all sat in a large circle and our model glided into the center of the room, whipping off his robe.

Yes, the first model was a man. I shouldn't even say man. He was more like a Greek god. He was completely bald and impossibly muscular. He looked like a real-life version of the superheroes I drew when I was a kid.

He was so muscular, he was able to hold his first pose for two and a half hours so we could do detailed drawings. His pose was an elegant reclining stance with his giant tree trunk legs splayed wide open so his crotch was pointing directly at me for *two and a half hours*. This was as close to a young attractive woman as I would get for years.

For the majority of my classes, the main model we worked with was an older woman, a pro who was super-casual. She would take off her robe and wander around naked to look at the pictures, get a drink of water, have a terrible coughing fit, talk to you about *The X-Files*, whatever. She was like your favorite aunt if your favorite aunt was always naked.

And then came gesture drawing day. In gesture drawings, you have fifteen seconds to make big sweeping movements across the page to try to capture the energy and flow of the model's pose.

I liked doing gesture drawings. Here's an example of what a gesture drawing might look like:

My favorite naked aunt was sick on gesture day. And she had a friend substitute.

A friend who dabbled in mime.

The second the mime walked into the room everyone became uneasy. He had bulbous twinkling eyes set deep back in his head, dark blonde hair with an awkward poof in the front and a creepy smirk like he just sold some old lady a broken down Cadillac or kidnapped a child.

He mounted the podium in the center of the room with a quick birdlike hop and announced, "I've never done this before!" Then he whipped off his robe like a master chef pulling the top off a platter and said, "Okay! Let's do this thing!"

As you'll recall from the beginning of the story, this mime had a tiny penis. Often in life we encounter men with a macho, aggressive attitude and we laugh, saying, "I bet this guy is just compensating for his tiny dick."

It is a very strange experience to physically see both the tiny penis and the compensatory attitude at the exact same time.

The model strutted and leered about the podium and our teacher calmly asked him to strike an exciting gestural pose.

Normal gesture poses are reaching hands skyward or a balletic pose like an arabesque. The creepy man pretended he was trapped in a shrinking box.

We all stared in horror. The entire fifteen seconds passed without a single person drawing anything. Our teacher asked, "So, uh, what was that?"

He said, "Oh, I'm kind of a frustrated mime," and suddenly he was being blown by a mime wind that he staggered against, his huge scrotum almost throwing him off balance.

It was indeed the worst three hours of my five-year college experience. It was made worse by the fact that it passed in fifteen second increments.

After that day, I questioned whether I really wanted to be a visual artist. Sure, I loved superheroes and comic books, but I was never very disciplined. I didn't like drawing crowd scenes or buildings and only sometimes bodies. I mostly just liked to draw faces. For example, here is a picture of what I remember the creepy mime looking like:

Besides, my favorite part of all my art classes was when we would have peer review. I would hang my drawings and paintings up and then have the captive attention of a room full of people. The teacher would have to remind me to actually talk about the pictures as opposed to make random jokes to try to get a laugh.

Did I really want to be a visual artist? Did I really want to go into a creative field filled with difficult odds? A field where it can be incredibly challenging to make a living?

No, I decided. That *Oliver Twist* experience in junior high was pretty awesome. I think I'll go into comedy.

GEEK TOPICS COVERED

❏ Superheroes ❏ Robin the Boy Wonder ❏ *The War of the Worlds* ❏ Charles Dickens
❏ Awkward Relationships ❏ *The X-Files* ❏ Quoting Abraham Lincoln Incorrectly

26

A WORD PROBLEM

Q: Captain Kirk and Captain Picard are in a room together. There is one window, no door, and four walls. If you were trapped in the same room, but you were exactly 57 feet away from both of them, and the room's ceiling was angled at exactly 26 degrees and you were able to run toward Captain Kirk and Captain Picard at a top speed of 3.7 miles per hour, which one of them would you rather have sex with?*

*The answer is not printed in the back of the book.
The correct mathematical answer can only be found in your heart.

GEEK TOPICS COVERED

☐ *Star Trek* ☐ Captain Kirk ☐ Captain Picard ☐ Math ☐ Sex

27

YOU ARE AN AWFUL HUMAN BEING!

YOUR ADVENTURE BEGINS!

YOU ARE SITTING AT YOUR DESK. YOU ARE WRITING A PIECE OF INTERACTIVE fiction. It's inspired by *Choose Your Own Adventure* novels, but hopefully not similar enough to be legally actionable.

"Hey," you reason out loud, "no one owns the concept of interactive fiction so fuck you, imaginary lawsuit."

You take a sip of whiskey and feel guilty about using the f-bomb. After all, you're writing in the second person. There's only so much one can assume about the character of "you."

Maybe "you" is a nun. Maybe "you" is a nun with a filthy fucking mouth.

The point is that much of the joy of reading second person interactive fiction is imagining that the main character is indeed you. Giving the character of "you" too many specific or distinctive traits (such as a filthy fucking mouth) risks alienating the reader.

You take another sip of Jameson from your favorite shot glass that your wife bought you in Scotland and push the lock of brown hair that always falls over your left eyebrow back into place.

That was probably too specific.

Writing interactive fiction is more difficult than you thought it would be.

You flip open the calendar on your desk and look at the entry for today. You've written these words in bright red ink:

MUST FINISH INTERACTIVE FICTION PIECE TODAY.
IF YOU DON'T YOU WILL BE TOTALLY FUCKED.
COME ON, SELF, MEET THIS DEADLINE!

You crack your knuckles and stare at the computer screen. You toy with the idea of taking a really short break from writing to just look at one or maybe two things on the internet.

If you make the personal decision to keep writing, visit page 141.
If you make the personal decision to look at the internet, visit page 139.

READ WHAT YOU KNOW!

YOU OPEN YOUR BROWSER AND LOOK AT FACEBOOK. MANY PEOPLE HAVE cats and opinions about politics. Some of their political opinions are expressed through pictures of cats with captions. Many of your friends are violently angry about changes to Facebook. They are using Facebook to easily communicate to as many of their friends as possible about why they don't like Facebook.

One of your friends has posted a link to an article about writing.

"Why," you say to yourself out loud, "reading about writing is almost as productive as writing itself!"

You click the link with pride and settle in for a good enlightening read. The article is really fucking long. It takes about ten thousand words to say this:

> There's no easy answer to staying productive as a writer, you just have to sit down and do the work.

The article then spends another ten thousand or so words to say this:

> Don't let yourself get distracted by things like reading articles on the internet.

You feel actual visceral pain, as if irony is giving you a wedgie.

That is it. You are going to write now.

"I'm not fucking around anymore," you say to no one.

You close the browser and start to type. You type this:

"Arrgh blargh farggh-dee-farggh."

You realize you can't write right now, because you are too *angry* about how much time you wasted not writing by reading that how-not-to-waste-your-writing-time article.

Clearly, the most productive thing to do is deal with the anger so you can return to your computer fresh and relieved. You will be so calm. You will be like white silk blowing by a window that's looking out on a peaceful beach. You will be a human tampon commercial and you will be happy about it.

You just need to find a way to deal with the anger. Your choices are clear: You can play a violent video game for catharsis or take a quick nap to dream the anger away.

Yes, these are both great ideas.

If you make the personal decision to take a nap, visit page 143.
If you make the personal decision to play a violent video game, visit page 147.

BRAINSTORM!

YOU PUT YOUR FINGERS ON THE WELL-WORN HOME KEYS AND TYPE. YOU immediately delete what you just typed because it's a bunch of nonsense. There's a small problem in that you haven't decided on a topic for your interactive fiction story.

You brainstorm a list of exciting pulp genre interactive fiction sounding titles:

Curse of Skeleton Lake

Attack of the Mountain Zombies

Oral Surgery!

Where in the World is the Sweet Tooth Yeti?

Swamp Monster on a Zeppelin

You Are A Lady Cowboy!

Quest for the Pirate Troll

Syphilis Train!

You remember that, according to all your oversensitive college writing teachers who reeked of patchouli and lack of ambition, there are no bad ideas in brainstorm mode. You leave brainstorm mode so you can openly admit all your ideas suck.

You want to write something that is fulfilling for you as an artist, but also something that will interest people. You don't want to write some boring indulgent piece of shit about your writing process or some bullshit like that. No, you want your interactive fiction story to strike a chord with the masses.

You decide to make a list of things that are really popular. You tear apart pieces of blank paper. You get a paper cut. You yell, "Son of a motherfucking ass monkey!" and suck on your finger. You feel pretty stupid and are really happy no one is watching.

You bandage your finger.

You spend hours writing down phrases and ideas on the torn pieces of paper. You write things like "social media," "bacon," and "ukulele." You put them all in a hat.

The specific kind of hat you put them in is a fez. You remember people really like fezzes so you put another piece of paper that says "fez" in the fez.

You reach your hand into the fez and swirl the pieces of paper. You get another paper cut. You look up at the ceiling and scream, "Why? Why? What the hell have I done to deserve this?"

You compose yourself and gingerly pull out four pieces of paper from the fez. You separate them so you end up with two pairs of two.

You will write a brilliant piece of interactive fiction about the topic generated by one of these ideas.

The first pair is: Steampunk Mummies

The second pair is: Vampire Ponies

It could be worse.

If you make the personal decision to write about Steampunk Mummies, visit page 145.
If you make the personal decision to write about Vampire Ponies, visit page 151.

NAPPED!

YOU LIE DOWN ON THE COUCH. YOU SET THE ALARM ON YOUR smartphone to go off in half an hour.

You have no doubt a nice, soothing nap will calm you down and get you in the right mood to write your interactive fiction story.

"Feed a fever, nap a rage," your mother used to say.

Your mom said a lot of weird things. You think of your mother and drift off to sleep.

You have strange and horrible dreams. You're sitting at your computer, but the keys aren't real. They're a wooden sculpture. Every time you press one the entire keyboard presses down and a message appears on the screen that says: "404. Fatal Error. You are an idiot."

Suddenly your mother appears in the window. You open it to talk to her. She says she can't talk right now because she had a new child. She is holding something wrapped in a baby blanket.

It is a rotting watermelon with eyes and a mouth.

Your rotting fruit sibling looks at you with pity and says, "Don't worry. Someday your life will smell better."

Your smartphone alarm goes off and you wake up screaming.

That was not relaxing at all. You debate whether to try

a second nap or just get up, go back to your computer, and start writing.

Everything smells like rotten fruit.

If you make the personal decision to return to writing your story, visit page 141.
If you decide to go back to sleep, visit page 153.

STEAMPUNK MUMMIES!

YOU WRITE AN INTERACTIVE FICTION STORY CALLED *TOMB OF THE Steampunk Mummies.*

It spins the tale of a successfully undefined second-person narrator who discovers an ancient Egyptian pyramid made almost entirely of gears. Here is an excerpt:

> With one final mighty yank on your crowbar, the large bronze door (inlaid with intricate brass detailing) creaks open. You suddenly find yourself face-to-face with the time-traveling pharaoh!
>
> He is wrapped head to toe in elaborate bandages with space for his piercing black eyes and his thin, cruel smile. He also has a top hat, a monocle, a sword cane, a vest with buttons that are just old typewriter keys, and an elaborate exoskeleton of grinding gears, pumping iron shafts, and two decorative cogs placed directly in front of his already bandage-wrapped nipples. None of this seems to serve any immediately obvious function.
>
> "Good evening," he says in an inexplicable British accent and then uses a crankshaft hooked up to a computer screen to post on his Twitter feed.

The Tomb of the Steampunk Mummies is a huge success. It becomes the best-selling interactive fiction story of all time.

Fans begin cosplaying *Steampunk Mummies* at conventions. Time after time, their mummy bandages get caught in their pointlessly spinning steampunk gears and they are throttled to death by their own costumes.

The book is pulled from the market. You are reviled as the world's first accidental mass murderer. You go mad with guilt. You spend the rest of your life alone in a small room with a deathly fear of any technology that has visibly moving parts.

Still, you are very proud that you actually wrote the damn story instead of spending that fateful day, lo those many years ago, dancing with a devil called procrastination.

THE END

LET'S KILL SOME PEOPLE!

YOU SIT DOWN TO PLAY YOUR FAVORITE VIDEOGAME. IT'S AN ACTION-adventure RPG FPS called *GoldenShooter*.

You play suave yet savagely violent secret agent Jack Thrust. The game features a complex, interactive fiction narrative about Thrust's quest to avenge the natural death of his elderly father. The tag line of the game is, "No one did it on purpose. Now everyone has to pay."

But you're not playing the game to enjoy the rich and thoughtful narrative about the nature of justice and mortality. You're playing to shoot some motherfuckers in the head. Luckily for you there is a mode in the game called "Shoot Some Motherfuckers in the Head Mode."

In this mode, you find yourself in a sprawling urban environment in which everyone has a weapon. Baby strollers are just cleverly disguised mobile grenades. Postal workers throw razor-sharp letters at your head. It is so super violent.

The game starts up. Your fingers steady on the well-worn buttons of the controller.

You select your favorite outfit for Jack Thrust (underwater tuxedo) and your favorite gun (a massive double-barreled shotgun with an attached double-barreled silencer for stealth missions) and hit the "Engage Death" button to begin playing.

You shoot people.

To your great annoyance, they shoot back.

You keep dying.

You get really frustrated. After all, you are playing this game to calm yourself so you can get back to writing your own interactive fiction epic.

The characters in the video game don't seem to understand this. You need them to put up enough of a fight that you feel like you're still accomplishing something, but not such a good fight that you can't easily win. Their artificial intelligence is supposed to be so advanced. Why don't they understand? You decide maybe they would understand if you screamed at your television.

You scream, "Just let me shoot you, you stupid fucking postal worker!"

Your outraged pleas stir up the neighbor's Chihuahua. It begins yapping.

You mash the buttons on your controller even harder and in an impressively perfect rhythm with your foul-mouthed tirade.

The internal fan in your game console kicks in. It whirrs obnoxiously. Even the fan seems exasperated.

You shoot. You die. The Chihuahua yaps. You scream. The fan sighs. A postal worker cuts Jack Thrust's head off with a letter from a cable company about bundling your services.

You lose control. You stand up and hurl your controller down on your coffee table. The glass of the coffee table shatters. One of the shards flies up and lodges in your throat severing your carotid artery.

You collapse to the floor and die.

All because you couldn't just sit at your computer and write your damn interactive fiction story.

THE END

VAMPIRE PONIES!

YOU WRITE AN INTERACTIVE FICTION STORY CALLED *TRIUMPH OF THE Vampire Pony.*

In your story, the ambiguous second-person narrator falls in love with a pony who also happens to be a vampire. Here is an excerpt:

> You mount Edmund. Normally, you couldn't ride a pony as small as Edmund, but Edmund is no ordinary pony. He is a vampire pony.
>
> You ride Edmund to the edge of the fence but he refuses to jump over. After all, it's a wooden fence. Every post is basically a stake waiting to pierce his pony heart.
>
> "Edmund," you plead, "we must escape!"
>
> It's true. You can hear the wild pack of angry werewolf donkeys howling and braying in the distance.
>
> "Please, Edmund," you say softly into his vampire pony ear. "If we escape now, we can put our hearts together and nothing will be able to pierce them ever again!"
>
> Suddenly Edmund rushes toward the fence and sprouts strange yet beautiful bat wings. You had no idea Edmund could turn into a vampire bat pony!
>
> Edmund launches himself over the fence and you soar into the air! You leave all of your problems behind—flying away from the werewolf donkeys, the zombie squirrels, and the sadness of Edmund's dark past.
>
> You circle the forest, crying with joy, knowing that your strange love will last forever!

It's really fucking weird, but it's a huge hit. *Triumph of the Vampire Pony* is filled with ludicrous dialogue and vaguely suggestive sexual subtext but since the identity, age, and gender of the second person narrator is so successfully ambiguous, no one can pin down an exact meaning.

The story spawns an entirely new genre of fiction called Ambiguous Love. You win the Nobel Prize in Literature as well as in a new category created specifically for you.

You win the Nobel Prize in Being Awesome.

All because you had the willpower to just sit down and write on that one fateful day. Awesome.

THE END

SLEEP OF THE DAMNED!

YOU GO BACK TO SLEEP. YOU DON'T EVEN BOTHER TO SET THE ALARM ON your smartphone.

This time, you hum softly to yourself. You rock yourself gently back and forth. You do not want to see the watermelon baby again.

It takes about fifteen minutes, but finally you are asleep.

It's a deep dark slumber.

You think you're aware of dreaming things. You're somewhere near the edge of a cliff, so you move away.

"Screw you, dream brain," you sleep-think, "I'm not falling for the old fall-in-the-dream-then-wake-up-in-real-life trick. I'm doing some hardcore sleeping, motherfucker."

And you do. Your eyes move rapidly but you are totally unaware of it.

Suddenly you are awake. There is a puddle of drool on the throw pillow. Your hair is sticking up at almost non-Euclidean angles.

You don't remember what day it is. You feel like you had something important to do. You struggle up and straighten your clothes. Your underwear is wedged up above your pants. You do an awkward dance to sort everything out as you walk into your office.

You look at your calendar. It says:

MUST FINISH INTERACTIVE FICTION PIECE TODAY.
IF YOU DON'T YOU WILL BE TOTALLY FUCKED.
COME ON, SELF, MEET THIS DEADLINE!

You look at the date on your computer.

You realize you have slept through the night and into the next day.

You have missed your deadline. Technically, you are fucked.

But you feel very rested and relaxed. You sit down at your computer and start to type. The words flow easily.

You write an interactive fiction story. It is not the story you should have written yesterday. It's a different story. It's a strange yet cathartic story called *Terror of the Watermelon Babies*.

You submit it to your publisher. It is rejected for being one day late.

But it exists. And you like it.

And maybe that's okay.

Maybe that's okay.

THE END

CONCLUSION!

I HOPE YOU ENJOYED READING/PLAYING *YOU ARE AN AWFUL HUMAN BEING*! Of course, you aren't actually an awful human being. We're all out in the world just trying our best. And sometimes we make choices that cause us to succeed, fail, or die suddenly.

Also you may think that the character of "you" in *You Are An Awful Human Being!* is pretty obviously me, Joseph Scrimshaw.

Nothing could be further from the truth. Only a few details are accurate. In the course of writing *You Are An Awful Human Being!,* I did drink a lot of whiskey, move a lock of brown hair off of my left eyebrow, swear a lot, play a video game, take a nap, and screw around on the internet.

Other than that, the story has no relation to my life whatsoever.

After all, I finished writing this book, didn't I? I did, right?

I hope this isn't a dream. If you are a watermelon baby, PLEASE DON'T TELL ME.

Thanks again,
Joseph "Not You" Scrimshaw

GEEK TOPICS COVERED

❏ Interactive Fiction ❏ Bacon ❏ Ukulele ❏ Fez ❏ Steampunk ❏ Mummies ❏ Vampires ❏ Ponies ❏ Werewolves ❏ Video Games ❏ Super Spies ❏ Social Media ❏ Non-Euclidean Angles ❏ Guilt

28
A DANGEROUS MISTAKE

Sometimes I get Order 66 and Rule 34 confused.

GEEK TOPICS COVERED
❒ *Star Wars* Prequels   ❒ Slash Fiction

29

THE HONEY BEAR RISES

I'VE SAID A LOT OF ALARMING THINGS TO MY MOTHER, BUT I THINK THIS is the one that scared her the most:

> Mom. I'm very depressed today. Today is the day that I've finally come to terms with the fact that I will never be a superhero.

In theory, it wasn't that terrifying of a thing to say. It clearly demonstrated that I had a firm grasp on reality. The problem was I said it when I was about sixteen years old.

I had been doing odd things because of superheroes virtually my entire life.

At the tender age of three, I threw my mother's vaguely web-shaped laundry basket over the landlord's head. You know, to be like Spider-Man. I was under the impression the landlord was a super villain because he kept coming around to get money from my father. On a perhaps related note, we moved across the country a few weeks later.

My mother used to watch reruns of *The Andy Griffith Show*. When Gomer Pyle shouted his catchprase "Shazam!" I would demand to know why he wasn't turning into Captain Marvel.

I was also exposed to soap operas at a young age. Soap operas and superheroes are a deadly cocktail in the mind of a child.

When I was four years old, my mother was babysitting the neighbor girl. I convinced my neighbor to play Superman with me. Even at four years old, I knew this was going to be an uphill battle. She eventually conceded to playing Lois Lane to my Superman. She asked the logical question, "What would Superman and Lois Lane do together?"

Thankfully, all those hours of staring at *All My Children* with my mother had prepared me.

"Look, neighbor girl," I probably said, "Superman and Lois Lane like each other, right? And what do people do when they like each other? They take their shirts off and cuddle really close to one another in bed."

And so we stripped and got under the covers. In my mind, the next thing that should've happened was a quick cut to a commercial for cleaning products or yogurt. Instead, I think we just dozed off. Thanks to Superman and *All My Children*, I was already boring women in bed by the time I was four years old.

Eventually, my mother took a break from raking the shag carpeting in the living room and popped her head in the bedroom. "So, uh, what are you doing?"

"What the hell does it looking like I'm doing, woman?" I probably didn't say, "I'm playing Superman!"

My mother caught me red-handed having unprotected napping with the neighbor girl. I could have been exposed to any number of virulent strains of cooties. But my mother wasn't terrified then. No, she thought it was cute.

Later that same day, I hid behind the couch and decided to act out more of Superman's personal life—this time inspired by overhearing my father's tales of employment woes.

In this exciting adventure, Superman's boss, Perry White, fired Clark Kent for showing up late to work all the time. I then had Superman punch Perry White so hard his head fell off. Both Superman and I felt very guilty about it.

I tried to tell my mother about it but she was skilled at tuning out the long rambling stories of my weird behind-the-couch adventures. They ranged from "I found a penny!" to "I punched a man's head off!"

But my deepest desire to be a superhero was instilled by one fateful conversation. In my mind, I was swinging through Gotham City looking for thugs to mercilessly beat. In practice, I was screaming and running in a random pattern that was totally unraking the shag carpeting. My mother offered this suggestion, as though it was an exciting idea: "Hey, why don't you go clean your room?"

I responded, "I don't see why anyone buys gum when they can just chew on their own tongue. See?"

(This is not *probably* what I said, this is *exactly* what I said and I have the tongue scars to prove it.)

She suddenly looked very intently at me and said, "I'm going to tell you something about Batman. You like Batman, right?"

I rolled my eyes with sarcasm beyond my years.

"Well, Batman doesn't technically have any superpowers. He just worked really hard to be the best person he could be."

In my adult life it has dawned on me that from my mother's perspective the moral of the story was, "I love you, but shut the fuck up and go clean your goddamn room."

However, this is what I heard:

"YOU SHOULD BE A SUPERHERO WHEN YOU GROW UP."

I retired to my room, did no cleaning, and made a mental list of what I would need to be a superhero. There were only two items on the list.

1. Get real strong.

2. Dress up like an animal.

Step one was no problem. I knew exactly how to get strong. I wasn't some idiot who hadn't spent the majority of his young life watching television. I knew the way of the world. All I had to do was wait until I was a little older and lift a barbell once or twice. This would cause non-diegetic music to kick in which would in turn start a brief montage of exercise. After a maximum of ninety seconds, I would be bulging with muscles.

But dressing up like an animal needed more serious consideration. I sat at my little drawing table. My brow furrowed. I chewed on my tongue, deep in thought.

I needed to eliminate the obvious.

What about a dog?

Our family pet was a small poodle named Dusty. (I believe my parents named my first pet Dusty because they really wanted that "What's your porn name?" game to work out well for me.) Dusty was a lot like Snoopy if Snoopy were clinically depressed. So I drew a quick picture of a sad dog costume. I realized being an emo poodle was just silly and crumpled up the paper.

I thought of dressing like a cat, but for some reason, I was under the impression that all cats were girls. Apparently, TV wasn't actually doing that good of a job at raising me. Plus, there was already a morally ambiguous super character named Catwoman. I didn't want to be CatwomanMan.

Being a superhero was serious business.

I considered Captain Goldfish, but I had an immediate fear of a super villain flushing me down a giant novelty toilet.

I looked out the window. I saw birds. Birds were stupid. All they did was sing and poop. I could do that. Big deal. Yes, they can fly. But I would never be able to do that. I wasn't fantasizing about actual super powers, I was dealing with *reality* now. This wasn't about fantasy, it was about working out for ninety seconds then dressing up like an animal to strike terror into the hearts of criminals.

Suddenly something leapt past my window. A squirrel!

Eureka! Squirrels were fast and athletic. I watched the squirrel for a while. Its main power seemed to be staring at things. I went into the kitchen and briefly stared at my mother. She didn't seem scared. Just exasperated. I didn't think I could exasperate a thug into stopping a bank robbery.

Then I saw it. Sitting on the kitchen counter. One of my father's empty beer cans. He drank a cheap beer called Hamm's. The beer's mascot was a bear.

A bear.

Bears were everywhere in my life. I had teddy bears. Smokey the Bear was always on television and in magazines preemptively scolding me for the huge forest fire I would inevitably cause if I ever went anywhere near a forest.

Yes, I would be a bear. But not a cartoonish, drunken, dancing fool like the Hamm's beer bear.

I would be a wild creature of the night. I would be terrifying. Like a shark, but on land. I would be Bear Man.

No. No, I wouldn't. That would make it sound like I was naked.

I would have to worry about the name later. I went back to my drawing table. Literally.

I sketched like a mad man, feverishly designing the costume. Once the muse had departed, I stepped back and looked at my drawing.

It was a picture of a large bear wearing a cape.

I added a thug shooting the bear. I circled the bullet bouncing off the bear to indicate the armor would be bulletproof under the fur.

I studied it more. It was a picture of a man shooting a teddy bear. Perhaps this would not inspire fear. Perhaps criminals would laugh at me.

Well, they wouldn't be laughing WHEN I SHOT THEM.

That's right, I was going to be a bear who carried a gun. Of course, I couldn't carry a real gun because superheroes don't kill people, they only hurt them very, very much. And so I decided I would carry a state-of-the art HONEY GUN. It would fire a burst of sticky honey to slow down my enemies so I could waddle over in my bear armor and slap them senseless like salmon in a shallow river.

I wasn't worried about where I would get the money to develop and produce bear armor and honey guns. That would be taken care of with a quick getting-rich montage.

When my older brother came home, I told him about my plan. I was open to him joining me in my adult career as an avenging bear of the night. We could be like Batman and Robin, except we would be equal partners. He told me we could work out the interpersonal power dynamics later.

We went outside and started asking the neighbor kids if they would like to join us in some sort of League of Terrifying Animals. I offered them my rejected animals: Captain Goldfish, CatwomanMan, the Human Squirrel, Sad Poodle.

These neighbor kids were so stupid they didn't grasp the basic concept of "get strong, dress up like an animal." One particular blowhard named Sean (a particularly popular blowhard name when I was a child) started spouting off about all the cool superpowers he was going to have when he grew up. Flight, invincibility, microwave heat rays from his eyes, etc.

We tried to pull him back to reality. I asked, "Yes, yes, but *how* in the *real world* will you accomplish this?"

He responded, "I don't know about the microwave heat rays but for flight, I'll get a jetpack and for being bulletproof, I'll just stick a piece of metal up my shirt."

We thought that was the dumbest fucking thing we had ever heard.

A piece of metal up your shirt? It was logistically stupid and, worse, it lacked drama.

I decided to teach him a lesson by talking. I painted the picture of how cool I would be as a bear-inspired superhero.

Picture it:

> There's a dark alley. A criminal is running around. I know he's a criminal because he's carrying a bag with a dollar sign on it.

Slowly, I emerge from the shadows. The first part of me that pops out is my big round bear belly. Then the honey gun. Then the unmoving bear face mask. Smiling. The bear is always smiling.

Before the criminal can react, I squeeze the trigger and the honey gun delivers its sticky payload: SPLORCH!

The criminal would struggle to free himself and he would stammer in terror, "Who? What are you?"

"Who am I?" I would answer, my voice deep and mysteriously not muffled by wearing a bear head. "I'm your worst nightmare. I am vengeance in a fuzzy, bulletproof suit. I am the Honey Bear."

The other kids stared at me.

"I think sticking metal up a shirt is probably cooler."

Idiots.

After that, we were more judicious with who we told about our secret crime-fighting goals.

As I grew up, I tried to hold on to the dream of being a crime-fighting bear, but other interests took hold. When I was a teen I became obsessed with the X-Men. The thought of being a mutant, being born into amazing powers, seemed tantalizingly real. There was a small part of me that hoped I would be sitting in biology class and suddenly microwave heat rays would shoot out of my eyes. Please, let it be my eyes. If any other body part suddenly shot out energy beams it would be incredibly embarrassing.

I started feeling weird about how often I fantasized

about having superpowers, so one day when my mother asked me what I was thinking, I made an incredibly odd choice for a teenager and told her the truth.

"Mom. I'm very depressed today. Today is the day that I've finally come to terms with the fact that I will never be a superhero."

She looked upset. Like I had made the shag carpeting of her mind go the wrong way.

"Well, uh, good. Good. You still know *Star Wars* isn't real, right?"

Clearly she had a lot of mental raking to do to put everything back in place.

The horrible super villain known as REALITY continued his vicious assault on my childhood fantasies.

I bought a weight set and the insidious lie of exercise montages was revealed. I would work out for hours and "Eye of the Tiger" never spontaneously played.

I gave up hope on becoming a mutant and almost entirely forgot about being the Honey Bear. I decided I wanted to be a comic book artist. Or maybe a painter. Or perhaps a drummer. Or an obnoxious avant-garde drummer who played the drums with paint brushes.

Eventually, I settled on being a writer and comedian. A career that would get me shot at just a little less than if I had become a superhero or a drummer who also paints live on stage.

"THE HONEY BEAR RISES"

The memories of my fervent childhood desire to dress up as an animal and fight crime came back to me when I was talking to a friend who leads a strange double life as a musician and an event planner. We were in a green room waiting to do a show. He gently strummed his guitar while telling me his latest adventure as an event planner.

"Here's what I tell people when I'm booking entertainment for an event: 'Sure, I could get you that guy, but why would you want that guy when I can get you BATMAN?'"

"Uh," I said. "I thought they wanted you to book a flamenco dancer?"

"They do, but I always say Batman because Batman is the best. He works the hardest. He never gives up. Why should they settle for anything less than Batman?"

As soon as he said this, I saw a bear in my mind. It took me a few days to make the connection. I had become so distracted by the superhero fantasy, I had forgotten the essential truth of what my mother had told me all those years ago.

"Batman doesn't technically have any superpowers. He just worked really hard to be the best person he could be."

And so, I've finally reconnected with the alarming fantasies of my youth. I've decided to take back what I said to my mother when I was sixteen years old. I want to be a superhero. I want to be the best at what I do. I want to be the BATMAN of being a writer and comedian.

While I now recognize it would be ludicrous to dress up as a bear to fight crime, I think dressing up as a crime-fighting bear would be a great thing to do for comedy.

Perhaps someday soon, you will be sitting in a dark theater. You will look up at the stage. And I will emerge out of the darkness. First my big round belly. Then my honey gun. Then my smiling bear face.

And you will scream out in terror, "Who? What are you?"

And I will answer, "Who am I? I am a dark avenging comedian with a firm grasp on reality. I am Honey Bear Man."

GEEK TOPICS COVERED

◻ Superheroes   ◻ Batman   ◻ X-Men   ◻ Superman   ◻ Catwoman   ◻ Lois Lane
◻ Spider-Man   ◻ Super Villains   ◻ Emo   ◻ *Star Wars*   ◻ The Horror of Reality
◻ Alcohol   ◻ Awkward Relationships   ◻ Watching an Abusive Amount of Media

"THE HONEY BEAR RISES"

30 HOURS OF CREEPY FUN

Here's something you can do to entertain yourself and really creep people out: Find a person who is nowhere near a computer and repeatedly yell at them, "Check your spam filters!"

GEEK TOPICS COVERED

❏ Spam   ❏ Tech Advice   ❏ Fun

31

BULLSHIT TIME

I've been a big geek about time travel for most of my life thanks to *Doctor Who* and *Star Trek* and the inherent desire that seemingly all people have to meet a dinosaur and kill Hitler. It's inevitable that if you spend a bunch of time thinking about time travel, over time you'll develop some strong opinions about the nature of time.

One of the things in life that always seems to take way too much time is dating. So I wrote this monologue about taking a short cut. It was part of an evening of short one-act plays performed in a bar. Audience members were eating and drinking and every ten minutes or so, a little bit of theater suddenly started up at a nearby table. If anyone decides to go to a bar and give this approach a try, please contact me and let me know how it goes.

EXCUSE ME! EXCUSE ME! MAY I HAVE EVERYONE'S ATTENTION FOR JUST A moment?

Hi.

My name is Evelyn and I am a single woman. I've been coming to this bar every night for the last week trying to meet that special someone. I've had dozens of blow-my-brains-out boring conversations with individual men. And I just don't have time for it tonight. I still have to go to the gym, grab some horrible fast food to undercut everything I just did at the gym, and then watch at least four hours of television so I'll have something interesting to dream about when I get my four hours of actual REM sleep before I get up and go back to work.

So basically, I need to save time by hitting on every man in this bar at once. And the ladies who are open to experimenting. I just want a life partner. I'm not picky. As far as I'm concerned a spouse is like a library card or a liberal arts degree: I probably wouldn't actually use one much, but I'd be embarrassed if I didn't have one.

Sooo, about me. I'm adventurous. Obviously. I am an excellent multitasker. I can do almost anything I set my mind to and bitch about it at the exact same time. I don't cook. I'd throw my refrigerator out but that would just be another part of the kitchen floor I'd have to clean. I like to laugh. Sometimes I feed my cat a saucer full of milk and Jameson and then film her trying to play bat the string. I'm not a bitch about it. I don't post it on YouTube or anything.

What else? I work for an office furniture company. I'm in charge of designing office clocks. I like to think that's my contribution to bringing the different demographics of the USA together: no matter who you are, how you vote, or where you live, chances are you've stared at a clock I've made and cursed it for not moving faster.

It's fair to say I have some issues with the concept of time. I call bullshit on time. Not even time itself, really, but all our bullshit rationalizations.

Time isn't a friend that accompanies us on our journey. Time is an annoying little jerk poking you in the back. Time is that cliché where you're driving a car and there's an obnoxious kid in the back going, "Are we there yet? Are we there yet?" That's what time feels like until you turn thirty or forty and suddenly that little shit in the back seat isn't saying, "Are we there yet?" She's saying, "You passed it! You passed it! You passed it!"

And there's no turning around. You can't whip a shitty on the highway of life. You miss the exit and you're screwed. You will never use the bathroom at that particular McDonald's. You just have to wait for the next one. Even though all the McDonald's kind of look the same, you'll never know if that was THE ONE.

Not that I'm comparing men to McDonald's. Sure, men can make you happy and fat and take years off your life, but they are inferior to McDonald's in one significant way: they do not change their menu or policies based on social or economic pressures. I'm not sure if that made sense.

I don't mean to be maudlin. I don't care about getting old. Crow's feet, love handles, cankles, turkey neck, the golden arches—you name the insulting term for the natural progression of the female body, and I couldn't care less if it's happening to me. I just don't want to get old without having all the stuff I want.

Which leads to the obvious question of what I want.

I want companionship. I want to have sex with a man, then wake up and be happy he's there instead of wishing I had an ejector button for the right side of my mattress. I want someone who won't be offended if I accidentally drop the f-bomb during our wedding vows. I want someone to come with me to the emergency vet when my cat's liver inevitably fails. I want someone who will lie to me and tell me it had nothing to do with the Jameson. And then laugh at his own bullshit.

I want someone who looks like Roger Moore but fucks like Sean Connery. Hell, he could even look like Woody Allen as long as he fucked like Sean Connery. I want someone who realizes that Woody Allen actually did play James Bond in that weird 1967 version of *Casino Royale*.

I want a man who will give me a baby. Like he'd step out for a pack of smokes and he'd come back and say, "Honey, I decided to pick up some pizza rolls for dinner and I adopted this baby so you don't have to deal with all that pregnancy crap."

I want a man who understands that I want the destination without all the damn travel.

Sooo, that's me. I guess if you could make it through my little presentation and you still want to date me, I'd probably say yes. I'd take you back to my place to meet the cat. I'd tell you to pick out the best of the James Bond films to watch on Blu-ray and see if you get it right. We'd make sure we can order a pizza without debating the toppings like it was a nuclear disarmament treaty.

There would be no sex that first night. At least not with you.

If everything went really well, I'd pick a fight with you over money just to make sure that's not going to be a problem. And after that, a hug. A nice warm make-up hug. Because no one ever got gonorrhea from a hug.

So, in closing, thanks for your time. Best of luck with your journeys and if you think I might be the right destination for you, just do what the television tells you to when you're drunk at 3 a.m. Don't wait! Call now! Supplies are limited and time is running out.

GEEK TOPICS COVERED

◻ Time Travel ◻ Dinosaurs ◻ James Bond ◻ Watching An Abusive Amount of Media
◻ Alcohol ◻ Pizza Rolls ◻ Awkward Relationships

32
A PANTS-BASED GOAL

My goal in life is to be like the Hulk's pants. I might fray a little bit, but I will stay up no matter what happens.

GEEK TOPICS COVERED
❏ The Hulk   ❏ Pants   ❏ Hope

33

THE INDIRECT ADVICE OF UTTER USELESSNESS

I've noticed that a lot of fantasy stories, even incredibly high-quality stories such as *Lord of the Rings* and *Harry Potter*, share DNA. There is often a quest. There is often a story of friendship tested by danger. There is always a young hero of destiny and a wise old guide. I've also noticed that the wise old guide is often an asshole who, out of either narrative convenience or just sheer douchebaggery, can't be bothered to spell things out clearly. To demonstrate this, I've written the beginning of my own little fantasy story. For legal reasons, it stars a young hero with a terrible burden named Frojo and his wise but vague mentor Mumblemore. Please enjoy.

A DIRE WARNING

FROJO SAT IN HIS COMFORTABLE STUDY SMOKING A PIPE FILLED WITH dried leaves. There were many details about the length of the pipe, the girth of the pipe, the texture of its grain, the tree from which it was manufactured, the social mores of the race of people who planted that tree many centuries ago, as well as the names of the various books in which these details were first written down.

That is just the pipe.

It goes without saying and yet it must be said anyway that the dried leaves in the pipe and their history, texture, flavor, and effects could also be described in excruciating detail.

Alas, the slow and meandering tempo of Frojo's world was violently disrupted by a loud bang and the sudden appearance of the wise old wizard, Mumblemore.

In sharp contrast to what one would expect based on his behavior, Mumblemore was not smoking anything.

"Frojo!" he shouted. "Stop what you are doing immediately and listen to me! It concerns your ring!"

Frojo leapt to his feet and extinguished his pipe. He could tell this matter was very serious.

"What? What is it?" Frojo asked, his large eyes getting even larger.

"You and indeed the entire world are in grave danger," said Mumblemore. "So let's make a sandwich."

Frojo blinked and said, "I thought you needed to tell me about my ring?"

Mumblemore put his hand on Frojo's shoulder and peered at the unlikely young hero over his glasses.

"You do know how to make a sandwich, don't you? Go into the kitchen, get a knife, follow your heart, and try not to die."

A TOTAL LACK OF EXPLANATION

FROJO WAS VERY CONFUSED. EVERY TIME MUMBLEMORE SPOKE, HE seemed to say less.

Mumblemore was now wandering about the study just sort of fidgeting with things for no apparent reason.

"But Mumblemore, what about the ring?"

"It's very dangerous!" Mumblemore shouted suddenly while playing with a tea cozy.

"Yes," Frojo said, annoyance creeping into his voice. "You said that."

"It's incredibly dangerous!" Mumblemore added, wagging the tea cozy at Frojo.

"I do actually understand that part."

"It's like…" Mumblemore seemed to search for words as though they were literally floating in the air above him. "It's like if the two most dangerous things you can think of had a baby. And then trained that baby to be extra dangerous. The ring would be *more* dangerous than that."

Frojo nodded his head in a vain attempt to hide his frustration. "Yes, okay. But what should I *do* about it?"

Mumblemore glared, "You should be very, very frightened."

"Yes!" Frojo's voice began to rise tremulously. "But what *productive* course of action should I take?"

Mumblemore threw the tea cozy into the air. It disappeared with a wave of his hand. He reached behind Frojo's ear and pulled it out again.

Frojo was really starting to lose his temper. He felt there was a fine line between a sense of whimsy and just dicking people around.

"Frojo, my friend, listen carefully because this is very important. Here is what you *shouldn't* do—"

"Oh for fu—" Frojo barely stopped himself from saying a severe word that has a long and tedious etymology we don't have time to get into at this point in the story. "What? What *shouldn't* I do with the ring?"

"Do not under any circumstances put the ring on." Mumblemore added a wink for some reason.

"I wasn't going to!" Frojo shouted.

Mumblemore rushed toward Frojo, his robes billowing and his eyes filled with sudden urgency. He spoke with great emphasis and showered Frojo with spittle.

"This is no time for frivolity, Frojo! You must not pick up the ring and slip it on your finger with the ease of a hot knife cutting through the butter for the sandwich you still haven't made me! Do you understand, Frojo? Do you?"

"Yes!" Frojo yelled as he backed away from Mumblemore. "Apparently, you want me to save the world by making you a sandwich while not wearing a ring and being terrified about it!"

"THE INDIRECT ADVICE OF UTTER USELESSNESS"

MORE OF THE SAME BUT NOW WITH SINGING

MUMBLEMORE'S SHOULDERS SLUMPED IN DEFEAT.

"I'm not getting through to you, am I?" He sighed and shook his head. "Perhaps you need to hear it in the form of a song? Oh, Mr. Tim? Mr. Tim BlahBlahBlahBaDeel? Are you there?"

Frojo looked around.

The door to his quaint home burst open. A large man dressed in a garish suit appeared in the doorway.

He doffed his top hat and raised his voice in song as though he were the happiest drunk the world had ever known.

Hey diddly ho! Ring-a-ding dildo!

The big, happy man danced a little jig and finished with jazz hands.

For some reason, the jazz hands angered Frojo the most. "'Ring-a-ding dildo'? Who or what the hell is this?"

"Why, this is Tim BlahBlahBlahBaDeel!" Mumblemore said, as if that was something everyone should know. "He's ancient and wise and sings little songs he makes up on the spot. Listen to this one about your destiny!" Mumblemore tried another wink. It was unclear if it meant something or he was just developing a tic.

Tim BlahBlahBlahBaDeel checked the area around him

to make sure there was enough space to dance. Then he cleared his throat and belted loudly.

When you're confused and don't know what to do,
Sing this song and think through the clue-diddly-clues!
Take the thing to the place where the evil looms,
Whip it out and throw it down in the crack of doom!
Doom, doom, diddly doom dildo!

Tim BlahBlahBlahBaDeel bowed. Mumblemore stared at Frojo.

"Well," said Mumblemore, "I think that was pretty clear."

Tim nodded his agreement and started humming to himself as he minced about the room trying out little dance moves.

Frojo exploded, waving his arms and jumping up and down. "No! No, it wasn't clear! It wasn't clear at all! Start from the beginning and explain very slowly like you're talking to a child or someone who is about to operate heavy machinery! Please tell me *exactly* what I'm supposed to do! Why the hell can't you ever do that? Are you even sure you're talking to the right person?"

Mumblemore scoffed. "Of course! Besides, it doesn't really matter! You unlikely heroes are all the same! You're brave but whiney, you resist help from friends, evil lords can see through your eyes, you have scars that burn—"

"I have a scar that burns?" Frojo interjected with alarm.

"Not yet, but you will," Mumblemore shrugged.

"What does that mean?" Frojo's eyes were bulging out of their sockets.

"Don't worry, you will survive," said Mumblemore trying to calm Frojo. "You have a secret power your enemy doesn't."

"What!?"

Mumblemore stared at Tim BlahBlahBlahBaDeel who was facing the wall while practicing a pop and lock move. "I don't want to spoil the surprise."

Frojo was now screaming like he had never screamed before. "WHAT? WHAT IS MY SECRET POWER?"

"I CAN'T TELL YOU!"

"WHAT IS IT?"

"I CAN'T!" growled Mumblemore

"COME ON!" Frojo squeaked with rage.

"IT'S LOVE," Mumblemore boomed, "IT'S LOVE, YOU DEMANDING LITTLE BASTARD! LOVE!"

There was a moment of silence. Mumblemore and Frojo glared at one another. A breeze came through the still open door. Some of Frojo's papers wafted to the floor.

"Really?" Frojo asked. "The special power that will save me is love?"

Mumblemore nodded.

The silence was rent by Tim BlahBlahBlahBaDeel's thunderous voice rising in song.

Love! O, love di-dee-doo-do-a-love-dildo-live...

"Shut the hell up!" shouted Frojo and Mumblemore in perfect unison.

Tim BlahBlahBlahBeDeel continued his song very quietly to himself as though he had OCD and would have to start over from the beginning were he not allowed to complete the song.

Frojo, the young hero of destiny, armed with basically no knowledge and burdened with frequent recriminations that he was not frightened enough, stared at the wise old wizard.

Mumblemore removed his wire-rimmed spectacles and cleaned them with a corner of his robe. He put the glasses back on and fixed Frojo with a stern glare.

"So. Can I have my goddamn sandwich now?"

Here ends the first part of The War of Not Telling People Simple Straightforward Things That Would Really Help Them Out.

The second part is called Two More Things I'm Only Going to Hint At.

The third, and final part, is called I'm Not Even Going to Tell You the Title of the Story, You'll Just Have to Figure It Out for Yourself.

THE END

GEEK TOPICS COVERED

❏ *Lord of the Rings*   ❏ Harry Potter   ❏ Filking   ❏ Smoking Something   ❏ Love

34
IDIOT MODE

Once, after playing *Goldeneye* on the Nintendo 64 for twelve hours straight, I walked into the middle of the street, saw a car coming, and reached in front of me to hit the pause button until I could figure out how I wanted to handle the situation.

GEEK TOPICS COVERED

▫ Video Games ▫ *Goldeneye* ▫ James Bond ▫ The Danger of Fantasy

35

SPACESHIP WHATEVER SOMETHING GO!

I haven't watched a lot of anime in my life, but what I have watched I've enjoyed tremendously. I find the worldbuilding aspect of anime particularly inspiring. A lot of Western art considers itself bold if it combines two ingredients like sci fi and westerns or vampires and the South. Anime barges into the kitchen, throws ingredients everywhere, and smashes the spice rack with a laser sword powered by the ghost of a monkey. In that spirit, I've built a short customizable anime story concept. Read and read again for different yet similar results!

SPACESHIP WHATEVER SOMETHING *GO!* IS THE STORY OF A BRAVE, **adventurous** (man/woman/cat-person) **named** (Dash/Jamie Steans/Meowynn) **with large eyes and wild hair.**

Our hero is on a mission of (vengeance/redemption/intergalactic grocery delivery). **There are many dangers in this business including attacks from vicious** (robot sorcerers/space pirates with sentient mustaches/insensitive teenagers).

But (Dash / Jamie Steans / Meowynn) **is well prepared because** (he/she/ambiguous alien cat-person pronoun) **travels** the (galaxy/universe/multiple universes with complex interlocking timelines) in the trusty rocket the *Spaceship Whatever Something*!

Of course, *Spaceship Whatever Something* is no ordinary rocket! It is the only spaceship in the sky that has (an actual talking face on the front of it/cannons that shoot out other smaller cannons/bucket seats)!

(Dash/Jamie Steans/Meowynn) **is a brave and experienced warrior who is always armed with** (a sword made of fire/a gun that fires emotions/three arms).

Should all of this exotic weaponry fail, (Dash/Jamie Steans/Meowynn) **can always rely on** (his/her/ambiguous alien cat-person pronoun) **faithful sidekick,** (Zan Tysor/Dr. Bunnyface/Scooter the Gender-Confused Cockatiel)!

(Dash/Jamie Steans/Meowynn) **has been friends with** (Zan Tysor/Dr. Bunnyface/Scooter the Gender-Confused Cockatiel) **since they both fought in the great war against the evil** (spider babies/laser monks/dragon grocers)!

(Zan Tysor/Dr. Bunnyface/Scooter the Gender-Confused Cockatiel) **is a constant source of** (wisdom/sarcastic humor/upsetting space diseases).

The crew of *Spaceship Whatever Something* **is rounded out by** (Travis/Gilly Woods/Swizzlebeef) **who is a** (giant/super-giant/mecha-super-giant) **robot that has the power to transform into** (a flower/a gun that shoots flowers/a lobster) **and enjoys eating** (sweets/the hearts of enemies/cheeseburgers)!

But the happy crew of *Spaceship Whatever Something* is about to be tested like never before when they encounter a creature more evil and random then they could ever imagine called (Hu'rrrgh/Vilderak/Steve)!

This vile creature is composed entirely of (tentacles/tentacles/tentacles)!

Can our heroes triumph?

Find out in three... two... one... *Spaceship Whatever Something GO!*

GEEK TOPICS COVERED

❏ Anime ❏ Cats ❏ Annoying Sidekicks ❏ Mad Libs ❏ Tentacles

36
LITERATURE WITH EMOTICONS

It was the best of times :)

It was the worst of times :(

GEEK TOPICS COVERED

▢ Charles Dickens   ▢ Emoticons   ▢ Dichotomies

37

BLINK BLINK BLANK

The first Kurt Vonnegut novel I read was *Breakfast of Champions* when I was in eighth grade. After I read it, I developed this opinion: If you accept that the world is a stupid illogical place, then the world suddenly makes a lot more sense. This has always given me a strange comfort. I also related to his elegant use of science fiction in novels. One of my high school English teachers told me Vonnegut's stories couldn't be taken seriously because they were full of silly aliens. I experienced perhaps my first bout of nerd rage. I tried to push up my glasses, but I ended up just touching the bridge of my nose because I forgot I now had contacts and said, "But he uses science fiction as *allegory*." She just rolled her eyes and walked away. "So it goes," I thought bitterly. Years later, I wrote this story for a group I perform with called the Rockstar Storytellers. Our assignment was to write in the style of our favorite author. Thanks, Mr. Vonnegut. Poo-tee-weet?

HERE IS WHAT I KNOW:

Algernon Grimshank was a human being on the planet earth.

Like most human beings on the planet earth he had the following problem:

He was very smart and yet most of the time he behaved like an absolute idiot. He knew for a fact that most people behaved like idiots, too, and he suspected most of them were smart enough to know he behaved like an idiot. And yet, he tried to pretend he didn't, which was of course a very idiotic thing to do.

Algernon Grimshank's personal idiocy manifested itself like this:

He told people he was a writer.

He would go to dinner parties and high school reunions and say things like:

"Yes, writing is who I am!"

"Yes, writing isn't about deadlines!"

"Yes, writing is about truth!"

"Yes, yes!"

Here was the truth:

On any given moment, on any given day Algernon would have vastly preferred to sit on his couch, eat frozen pizza, and stare at a television than lift one finger to do anything even remotely productive.

Many of the idiots on planet earth felt this way. But they all thought it was very important to lie to one another about it.

And so Algernon Grimshank spent a ridiculous amount of his short life staring at things that were blank: pieces of paper, his computer screen, his friends' faces when he told them his story ideas.

Blink blink blank.

Over the years, older wiser idiots had taught Algernon many glib, cliché catchphrases that would help him become a truthful writer.

One of those phrases was this:
Write what you know.

Here is what Algernon Grimshank knew:
Laziness. Horrible soul-crushing sloth. So one day he decided to write about that. He did research on his subject by looking up sloth on a website called wikipedia.org.

Wikipedia was an online encyclopedia that any yahoo could edit. Many well-educated idiots doubted its truthfulness when compared to a real encyclopedia that could only be edited by a handful of highly trained yahoos.

This is what the ambiguously educated collective of yahoos knew about sloth:

It is a cardinal sin. Like murder, it merits damnation in hell without the possibility of forgiveness. Algernon found it odd that if you plan on killing another human being but don't really get around to it, you are just as likely to go to hell as if you actually slit someone's throat.

Blink blink blank.

Next the website told him sloth was sometimes associated with goats and the color light blue. He noted that a citation was needed.

Then the website told Algernon something so idiotic he doubted its truthfulness.

It said:

"Each of the seven sins is paired with a patron demon. The patron demon of Sloth is Belphegor. A demon who was sent from Hell by Lucifer to find out if there really was such a thing on earth as married happiness."

The website also told Algernon that Belphegor was

Hell's ambassador to France.

Furthermore, the website told him that Belphegor tempted humans to be slothful by creating ingenious bits of technology which would waste their time.

Like all demons, Belphegor could only be summoned to earth by throwing a sacrifice of some kind on the floor of your home. The sacrifice required by Belphegor was this: shit.

This caused the following sentence to pop into Algernon's brain against his will:

The mystical portal between Hell and France is poop.

Finally, the website told Algernon that Belphegor was traditionally pictured as an old man sitting on a toilet. Algernon Grimshank never knew that traditional Judeo-Christian demons were this lowbrow.

He was curious. He looked around his home for something akin to a big piece of shit.

He picked up a copy of his latest half-finished story and threw it on the floor.

POOF! A puff of acrid smoke filled the room and Algernon found himself in the company of an old man on a toilet.

The toilet-man said, "Hey, buddy! I'm Belphegor! What can Belphegor get for you? Don't just stare at Belphegor! Belphegor is here to help you. You got any questions for Belphegor?"

Algernon threw open the wardrobe of his mind and desperately searched for a few words that might go well together. He said, "Why are you sitting on a toilet?"

Belphegor responded: "It's like sitting on the truth!"

Blink blink blank.

"Look, Belphegor made something for you, buddy!"
The demon reached a wrinkled hand into the toilet and threw something to Algernon.
It was this:
A light blue Nintendo 3DS portable video game system. Belphegor pulled one out for himself. The game loaded in both devices was Tetris. They both began to play.

This is how you play Tetris:
You stare at a blank screen. Eventually different geometric shapes fall from the sky. You use your thumbs to jostle buttons so you can make the shapes connect with one another. Once the connected shapes form a complete line they disappear.
You can't win at Tetris. It's just a question of how long until you fail.

Hours passed. Belphegor yelled out things like:
"Yes, I just flipped the L-shape!"
"Yes, I just made six hundred and sixty-six lines disappear!"
"Yes! Yes!"

Algernon was enjoying himself. His eyes burned and his thumbs ached. Pieces of half-digested pizza fell in his gut, piling up into a mass of twisted geometric spires. He felt like an idiot. He should be writing, creating. He wanted to make all his words connect and form lines so he could win his next high school reunion.

He was all conflict and no resolution. His story really should end there. Instead, I am going to do something glib and cliché. I am going to insert myself, as the author, into the story. It's a lousy trick that reeks of postmodernism.

Here is what I know about postmodernism:
It's an ambiguous term that educated idiots like to bicker about at cocktail parties. We are currently trying to look smart by debating whether or not postmodernism is dead. It's difficult to decide since none of us can agree on what postmodern meant in the first place. Personally, I think it means to have the creator comment in a knowing way on his or her own narrative.

So with a poof of light blue smoke I enter the room with Algernon Grimshank and say this:
"Hey buddy, I'm your creator! How can I help you? What can I get for you? I'd like to resolve your problems as neatly and quickly as possible."
Algernon stares. Blink blink blank.

Belphegor tries to throw me my very own Nintendo 3DS, but I'm ready for him.

Wikipedia told me the secret to defeat the demon sloth: zeal.

Each of the seven deadly sins is opposed by one of the seven virtues: chastity, moderation, generosity, charity, humility, meekness, and zeal. Putting them all together, they don't make a lot of sense. I would not want to be in a room with a generous, humble, moderate zealot meekly offering to give their chastity to charity.

Eager to save my protagonist from himself, I launch into a zealous tirade! I say things like:

"Yes, you've got to write for yourself, not for anyone else!"

"Yes! Writing is like a fire in your soul and you must release it or you will get burned!"

"Yes! Writing isn't about coming up with answers, it's about asking questions!"

"Yes! Yes! YES!"

A huge flushing sound fills the room and Belphegor swirls into thin air, sucked back to Hell. Or France. Yes, let's go with France. Yes.

Finally, Algernon and I are alone together.

He asks the question we idiots rarely ask one another.

He says:

"Did you mean all that or did you just say that because you thought it would impress me?"

Eventually, these words fall out of my mouth and form lines:

"I want to say whatever I have to so I can win this story."

Algernon asks, "But why?"

I answer: "So I can tell myself that I've done something today. Once I've done something I can go home. I can sit on my couch and watch hours of television while complaining about how shitty the writing is."

Algernon asks:

"Will that really make you happy?"

I do my best to answer him truthfully.

I say:
Here is what I know.
Here is what I know.
Here is what I know.

GEEK TOPICS COVERED

☐ Demons ☐ Tetris ☐ Wikipedia ☐ Sloth ☐ Zeal ☐ Nintendo
☐ Watching An Abusive Amount of Media ☐ Correcting People ☐ Frozen Pizza

38
DYSTOPIAN KEGGER

Ain't no party like a dystopian future party, 'cause there are probably no parties allowed in a dystopian future.

GEEK TOPICS COVERED
❏ Dystopian Future ❏ Parties ❏ Poor Rhyming Skills

39

DATE NIGHT (IN MIND-BLOWING 3D)

SEX AND MOVIES HAVE ALWAYS BEEN IN BED TOGETHER.

Modern blockbusters are full of lantern jaws, heaving cleavage, and trunks bursting with junk. Even robots from space have testicles.

In fact, if Hollywood could get away with it, they would release a movie simply called *Pretty People Doing Sex*. And it would probably be a tear-jerking drama about poverty in third world countries. It would be followed up with the sequel *Pretty People Doing Sex II: The Fight for Uganda*.

But movies are tied to sex on an even more intimate level. Movies have always been aphrodisiacs. We used to go on dates to see movies in theaters with the hope of having sex. Probably not right there in the theater, but maybe.

Movies used to set the tone of the date. There was a romance to it: The flickering lights, the subtle ambient whirr of the projector, the intimacy as you sat in small seats, cuddled close, hands meeting innocently in the warm bag of butter-slathered popcorn. A comforting amniotic feeling washed over you and you were taken to another time and another place.

But not now.

Now the speakers are designed to make everything as loud as possible. Just try to share the wonderful intimacy with your date as a fart sound effect rips through the speakers with so much force you can feel it in your sternum.

A fart in your sternum.

Sexy.

Even when the movie is loud enough to wake the dead, your focus is still drawn away from the film by the sudden blast of a pop song. Some jackass left their embarrassing ringtone on full volume and now it sounds like a former winner on *American Idol* is singing to the whole theater from inside this jackass' pants. You look around for this jackass and realize it's you. You are the jackass with the obnoxious ringtone.

So you turn to apologize, but your date is about twenty feet away from you. Yes, technically, you're sitting in the next bucket seat over, but you're separated by a giant armrest stuffed with disgusting, overpriced, food-like products.

$8 hot dogs that are made of pork and dead birds and shame.

A $28 plastic bin of nachos with a vat of fake cheese so large, you could fall into it and become a super villain. After all, the cheese stuff uses the exact same chemicals as the lubricant on the condom in your back pocket that you won't be using tonight.

You can't even see your date clearly because you're both wearing giant freakish 3D glasses so you can really experience the thrill of those space robot testicles flying off the screen and landing right on your face.

Yes, thank you 3D films, for legitimizing the oldest anti-sex excuse in the world. Thanks to 3D films your date really does have a headache.

But going to a theater isn't even how most of us experience movies anymore.

We get them mailed to us. We devour superhero movies and dinosaur movies and dinosaur superhero movies. Meanwhile, Oscar-nominated films linger on our coffee table. We keep meaning to watch *Pretty People Doing Sex III: Plight of The Indonesian Orphans* but we've heard it's just too damn sad.

So we start watching a TV show. We don't even need to get the discs, we can stream it directly through our televisions. We can watch *Crime & Justice: Sexy People Who Get as Close to Actual Sex-Doing as is Allowed on Broadcast Television* any time we want. We can watch all 500 seasons in two sittings.

And we do.

It's the entertainment equivalent of an all-you-can-eat

buffet. And when I think sexy and romantic, I think, "Hey, baby, let's strap on a bib and eat germ-riddled pasta until we are so bloated, our eyeballs are distended."

Sexy.

We don't even need to be on a date or in front of a television anymore. We can stream movies and television shows directly to our phones and our tablets. You can find yourself alone in a bathroom with your iPad and the mood strikes. Suddenly you are sitting on the toilet watching *Citizen Kane*.

Your date or your spouse wonders what the hell you're doing in there for two hours until you reach the climax and exhale, "Rosebud!"

Movies have gone from a romantic date to a crass analogy for masturbating. I don't think it's healthy to spend all of your time alone in the bathroom watching *Citizen Kane*.

I want movies to be romantic again.

I don't want them to be a booming exclamation point. I want them to be a whispered ellipsis. I want them to be an invitation to a different time and a different place.

Somewhere a little sexier than reality.

Somewhere a little sexier than my bathroom.

GEEK TOPICS COVERED

❑ 3D Movies   ❑ Dinosaurs   ❑ Doing Sex   ❑ Space Robots
❑ Super Villains   ❑ Watching an Abusive Amount of Media

40
FREE ADVICE ABOUT LIFE

Keep things physically in perspective. Do not move toward small objects if you don't want them to become large.

GEEK TOPICS COVERED
▫ Science

41
INTERNET COMMENTS OF A SAD VAMPIRE

The following is a lengthy comment left on the website Vamptainment.com, a specialty site covering exciting news in the wide world of vampire movies, TV shows, novels, online memes, and even exotic merchandising such as Japanese body pillows with pictures of famous vampires in sexy poses. The vampire of lore first came to light in Bram Stoker's epistolary novel Dracula. *Could this ranting internet comment be the sign that vampires are actually real? You decide.*

DEAR ASSHATS,

My name is Samuel. I am a frequent reader of Vamptainment.com. I am very interested in the subject of vampires. Probably because I am one and have been for over two thousand five hundred years.

Vampires, of course, are not supposed to reveal themselves to mortals by doing things like posting pissy comments on shitty entertainment blogs, but I don't care. It's late and I've got a contact buzz from drinking a guy who just drank a half a bottle of tequila.

Also, I just broke up with girlfriend number eight thousand three hundred and eighty-seven. I really thought she was going to be "the one for a few decades until she dies" but, yet again, it didn't work out.

"Why didn't it work out?" no one bothers to ask. Well, I'm going to tell you.

Because if the internet isn't for answering rhetorical questions that haven't even been asked, then I don't know what it's for.

There comes a point in any relationship when you have to lay your cards on the table. I always get to that point where I have to tell a woman I'm a vampire. The woman is always really excited because she *thinks* she knows what a vampire is because she's seen all the movies and read all the books and has one of the body pillows.

The vampire, in popular culture, has basically become a grab bag. Take what you like, leave the rest behind. Mix and match like you're putting together a quirky outfit for a dinner party! Go crazy! Make it your own! Express yourself with your personal vampire experience!

Bullshit.

I'm going to tell you the truth about vampires.

Vampires are horrible undead monsters.

It used to be that when I approached someone in a dark alley and I was like, "Sorry, but I'm a vampire," people would start weeping and screaming, "Oh God, please don't kill me, I've done nothing with my life, give me five minutes," and all that.

But now they're just like, "OMG. Do you sparkle?"

The answer is yes. Yes, vampires do sparkle in the sunlight. If you consider bursting into flames and dying the one true death a form of sparkling.

That whole *Twilight* movie is nonsense. I watched that thing and I felt like I was watching a YouTube video of a thirteen-year-old girl describing what she thinks the plot of *Dracula* might be. It's just ridiculous.

Even "old" vampire movies are not accurate. The original Bela Lugosi *Dracula* movie has that weird "blah!" sound. Vampires don't go "blah!" I hate "blah!" It sounds like someone Auto-Tuned a belch.

And not all vampires come from Transylvania. If you're one of these people who think all vampires *have* to come from Transylvania, you're basically a vampire racist. We're everywhere. Get over it. The only vampires who wear capes these days work at the renaissance festival. Move on.

Also, vampires can absolutely see themselves in mirrors. That is why we all have such great metrosexual hair. Vampires don't appear in pictures, though. So if you ever see someone's profile pic and it's just a smartphone floating in front of a bathroom mirror, that person is probably a vampire.

The Dracula myth is also responsible for everyone thinking vampires are afraid of garlic and religion. If that were true there would be no vampires in Italy.

Here's the thing about religion: If you shove a cross in my face, yes, I will recoil. It's not that I'm so unholy that I can't bear the symbol of Christ. It's just that vampires are extra sensitive to proselytizing.

So, yeah, when you shove a crucifix in my face, it's uncomfortable. It's like a million Jehovah's Witnesses coming to my door at once. It's unsettling.

As far as the garlic thing goes—look, we have choices. There are a lot of people in the world. We can break into anyone's home and drink their blood. We can break into an efficiency apartment complex. That's like the vampire equivalent of buying in bulk at Costco. Apartment complexes are just giant human being happy meals.

So when I have the choice between gorging myself at an all-you-can-eat human buffet or going to the garbage house where the paranoid old European hoarder has put up garlic and crosses everywhere, yeah, I choose to avoid that house.

It is true that vampires can't enter places without being invited. But Facebook invites count, so vampires can pretty much go anywhere now.

It's also true that vampires sleep in coffins. Sleeping in coffins is like the vampire version of Easter.

You know, it's like someone said, "Hey, what if we made

Easter all about giant rabbits? And then we'll hide eggs, which don't even come from rabbits, and we'll make children look for them, and then reward them by giving them giant chocolate effigies of bunnies that they can eat until they puke. Blah."

Sleeping in coffins is EXACTLY like that. In that it makes no fucking sense but it's tradition, so you're the weird one if you don't do it.

Vampires and humans do have stuff in common. A lot of the same things that kill you also kill us. Being lit on fire, getting our heads cut off, high cholesterol, getting stabbed with wood.

And you know when you say "stabbed with wood," that sounds like it should be hard to do. But there is a lot of wood in this world. IKEA is a fucking death trap for vampires.

But we're pretty strong and we're pretty fast. Some of us can fly, others can hop pretty high. Some of us can turn into bats, some of us can turn into wolves. Really lame vampires can turn into a fine mist. Scary, right? I'm a dark creature of the night, here's my impression of a Febreze commercial. Bad ass.

I'm not really one to talk, though. My powers are not very impressive. I can read minds, but only the minds of very stupid people. It's not a power with a lot of practical applications. If you're sitting next to a stupid person and you're watching *Jeopardy!*, you can find out what the wrong answer is. Besides that, I don't know.

I can also hypnotize people. Obviously, that's a hard power to demonstrate over the internet. But who knows, maybe it will work?

> You can't look at my eyes, so think about my eyes.
>
> Think about looking into my big, blue, sad eyes.
>
> Now you start to have a sexy dream.
>
> Perhaps you touch yourself on the neck or the mouth or the elbow.
>
> Wherever is erogenous for you. I don't judge.
>
> You start to moan.
>
> Then you moan some more.
>
> You get up and walk over to your bedroom window.
>
> You are still moaning.
>
> You are moanwalking.
>
> You open your bedroom window.
>
> Hopefully it is large enough for me to fit through because I can't turn into a bat.
>
> If your window is too small, I will just have to go to someone else's house.
>
> Anyway, the point is that, in theory, I would come in and bite you now and it would be *sexy*.

Okay, if you're hypnotized, snap out of it. Don't be hypnotized anymore.

So, yeah, that's what vampires do. And I think that's why humans are so fascinated with us. It doesn't matter how you portray us—monsters or heroes or bad boyfriends—

we'll always be tied up with sex and sexuality. It's a weird intimate act to break into somebody's house and then bite them for a while. Honestly, sometimes I hypnotize someone into opening their bedroom window and then realize I'm not hungry. I'm just lonely. So I spoon the person for a few minutes and leave.

Wow. I've never written that down before. I always thought spooning was less creepy than bloodsucking, but I think I might be wrong.

Look, it's an *incredibly* lonely existence being a vampire. And the older you are, the sadder you get. I am a very sad vampire.

I sleep all day and mostly just sit up alone all night watching television. DVR has only been around for a little while. Before that it was all infomercials. That was my whole life: creepy cuddling and twenty-minute-long advertisements for technical colleges.

Of course, TV is pretty damn new. Back in the old days, I used to just sit in the middle of some European farmer's field and listen to crickets. Then I would see how many crickets I needed to murder before it got quiet. I had to be very careful to actually murder the crickets instead of turning them into vampires.

That's another hard vampire truth. We can totally turn animals into vampires. I've turned a lot of animals into vampires just to see if it would work. I've made vampire cows, vampire squirrels, vampire ponies. Quite a few vampire ponies, to be honest.

See? It's things like this that made me want to write this post. People need to know the TRUTH. You humans spend so damn much time thinking about vampires and I just think it's good to really *think* about the things you think about. I think you should be like, "Vampires? What's that about?"

You know?

Anyway, now that I've sort of blah'ed it all out, I guess what I'm trying to say is vampires aren't that different from you.

We need to eat. We're obsessed with sex. We get really pissed off when a Joss Whedon show gets canceled. We want love. We want to cuddle. Sometimes, we are horrible monsters. Sometimes we are bad boyfriends. We really want our hair to look nice.

And sometimes we get drunk on a guy who was drunk on tequila and post things we shouldn't on the internet.

Anyway, I think I'm going to order a body pillow and go to sleep.

Hugs,
Samuel
The Sad Vampire

GEEK TOPICS COVERED

❏ Vampires   ❏ Japanese Body Pillows   ❏ IKEA   ❏ *Jeopardy!*   ❏ Dracula
❏ *Twilight*   ❏ Joss Whedon   ❏ Watching An Abusive Amount of Media
❏ Alcohol   ❏ Vampire Ponies   ❏ Online Comments

42
SCHRÖDINGER'S JOKE

In theory, I both do and do not have a joke about quantum mechanics existing in my head right now.

GEEK TOPICS COVERED

❏ Schrödinger's Cat   ❏ Quantum Mechanics   ❏ My Geek Head

43

AN OLD HOPE

I'VE MADE THOUSANDS OF *STAR WARS* JOKES IN MY LIFETIME. THERE are at least five thousand references to *Star Wars* in this one book. I think it's also fair to say that *Star Wars* jokes make up roughly 97 percent of the content on the internet. *Star Wars* has been mashed up with zombies and Legos and I'm pretty sure there are zombie *Star Wars* Legos. If those don't currently exist, they will by the time you are done reading this sentence.

There. They exist now.

But my favorite *Star Wars* joke is something that really happened.

When the film came out in 1977, the toy company was so blindsided by its success they didn't have time to actually produce action figures for the Special December Time Holiday Consumerism Extravaganza. So they advertised an empty box. The idea was that kids would buy the box now and then the company would send you some *Star Wars* action figures to stick in the box someday.

Amazingly, kids successfully harassed their parents to buy an empty box. The toy company sold a promise that could have ended up a lie. Thousands of children across the country were acting out the plot of *Waiting for Godot* and they didn't even know it.

But the toys did come and they were well worth the wait.

In 2005, the final *Star Wars* film came out. In the intervening time, a lot happened to the *Star Wars* franchise. It started out a young hopeful boy on Tatooine. Then at some point Obi-Wan Kenobi cut its arms and legs off and left it burning by a lake of lava. Now it was Darth Vader. It was still awesome but it was scarred.

To celebrate the release of *Revenge of the Sith,* the toy company did a special commemorative reissue of the empty box. Again, there were no actual action figures inside. But this time the box came in a box so collectors had to buy two boxes—one to keep the box in the box and the other to take the box out of the box so they could actually play with the box.

At the time, this seemed like a good analogy for the *Star Wars* phenomenon: Grown men and women repeatedly buying something that beneath all the layers had become, essentially, empty.

Star Wars was the first movie I ever saw in a theater.

I don't remember seeing commercials for the action figures. I don't remember being subtly manipulated to want a cheap plastic statue of Harrison Ford with a freakishly misshapen head. I just did.

I figured out the basics of life and death playing with

Star Wars action figures. When my grandfather died, I understood what happened because Obi-Wan had died in *Star Wars*. I knew that when my grandfather had a heart attack, he disappeared and his clothes wafted down onto the Barcalounger.

My mother was quick to assure me that wasn't actually what happened when people died. She said their bodies stay here but their souls disappear and go to heaven.

"Okay," I said. "Where's heaven?"

"It's, uh, it's up," said my mother.

I was thrilled to hear this. I went to my room. I put my Obi-Wan Kenobi action figure on the top bunk of my bunk beds. I put my Luke Skywalker action figure on the bottom bunk. I had Luke throw his grappling hook up to Obi-Wan so he could climb down and come back to life.

My *Star Wars* action figures and I had solved the problem of *death* and it wasn't even lunchtime yet.

But *Star Wars* figures did not lie. They quickly taught me the true pain of loss.

I was getting in the right mood to be the ring bearer for my aunt's wedding by playing with my stormtrooper action figure in the kitchen. I took his little plastic blaster out of his hand and started holding it near the sink.

I was fascinated that something that meant that much to me could so easily slip down the drain. Of course, it did.

Being a child, I was still able to be utterly shocked by the obvious.

I screamed and cried. Even as my father tried to comfort me, I remember feeling sorry for him because he couldn't figure out why the hell I was that upset over a little piece of plastic molded in the shape of a space gun.

By the time *The Empire Strikes Back* came out, I was much more savvy. My brother was a bitter man of nine years old. He warned me there was always the possibility we wouldn't get *Star Wars* toys for Christmas. I was terrified at the thought of getting traditional, *non-branded* toys. I didn't want to play with a wooden truck or a chemistry set with no movie tie-in or pre-existing narrative to inform my playtime adventures.

The previous year I had watched in horror as my cousin got a horse head on a stick. A horse head on a stick was not a toy. That was a threat from a mobster.

Luckily, I got a $3\frac{3}{4}''$ action figure of Princess Leia in Hoth fatigues. She was exactly what I wanted. I'm a little disturbed that what I wanted when I was a child was a small cold woman, but I was a weird kid.

Weird kids the world over got a huge gift in *The Empire Strikes Back*: Yoda. Technically, he was an ancient Jedi master. But from my perspective, he was me. He was short, odd, he talked funny, and he liked to poke at people with a stick. Secretly he was wise and powerful, just like every weird kid wants to be.

After Christmas, my mother took me to the toy store. We had to ride a bus, walk half a mile, and then take another bus. She kept calling me a trooper. I was proud and also annoyed that she kept leaving the "storm" off.

Other kids on the block had spread rumors in hushed reverent tones that this particular department store was the city's answer to Dagobah. They claimed I might find an elusive action figure of Yoda hiding there. Much like Christmas, my brother had braced me for the hard truth: "It will probably just be a bunch of Lobots."

When I turned the corner of the toy aisle, I screamed. It was a lousy bunch of Lobots. Plus one Yoda hanging on the lowest rack. As a jaded adult, the closest I can come to fully recalling that feeling is when I think I'm out of beer, but then find one lurking in the back of the refrigerator. It was like that times a million.

Yoda was a treasure. He elevated my status on the block. Every time my brother wasn't around, an older kid would try to talk me into trading Yoda for *all* of his *Star Wars* action figures. It was so tempting. I wanted to collect them all. But I knew that trading Yoda would be giving away something special. The film had taught me not to take the quick, easy, seductive path, so I would just stare at the older kid for a little while then suddenly run away like a little human squirrel.

Besides, the older kid was not delicate with his action figures. He moved their limbs too much, too often, and too aggressively.

"His Princess Leia in Bespin gown is so loose," I would say, having no idea what it was I was actually saying.

The years between *The Empire Strikes Back* and *Return of the Jedi* started to stretch on and on. When I wasn't playing with action figures, I was reaching out my hand to try to move things with my mind—books, sticks in the yard, kids at school I didn't like, the 45 record of Al Yankovic singing *Yoda*.

My brother and I debated endlessly about how the plot would resolve. Would the rebels overthrow the empire? Would Luke become a Jedi and kill Darth Vader? Was Lando Calrissian really that big of an asshole?

By the time *Return of the Jedi* was released, I myself was a bitter young man of the world. I was well aware that by the time I was in my thirties, half the world would be dead from AIDS, nuclear war, or maybe just razors in Halloween candy.

It was kind of a frightening time to be a child.

There was a general sense that the future would bring certain doom and the only real question was what shape that doom might take. So it was amazing to sit in the movie theater and see things actually start to work out for my rebel friends.

I vividly remember staring at the screen (not eating my Junior Mints in case they were poisoned) and watching Luke use his FULL JEDI POWERS to rescue Han. Then Leia was on screen.

So much Leia.

There she was throttling Jabba the Hutt all by herself.

Then I watched the Ewoks prance around and I felt... I didn't have a word for it. Confusion? Betrayal? Prepubescent ennui? The shuddering horror at the death of my childhood? I don't know. I didn't like the Ewoks.

You have to understand the original *Star Wars* trilogy is like a relationship.

The first chapter is exciting and new.

The second is dark, mature, and complex.

Then in the third chapter there are furries.

I was not okay with this. I had teddy bears and I had action figures. I had the good sense to keep them apart. Why didn't George Lucas?

But then came the climax in which Luke becomes a Jedi by refusing to fight. I had played out this scenario with my action figures a thousand times and never once did it occur to me that he wouldn't just take his lightsaber and cut his father's head right the hell off.

I discovered the concepts of pacifism and redemption before I even learned the words.

It was really annoying.

It was hard to craft an exciting story with your action figures once Luke was all-powerful and really kind. You might as well break out your Gandhi action figure and your Dalai Lama with the no-kung fu grip and just have them stare peacefully at one another for a while.

But that is the way of the Jedi. That is the way of the Force.

These are my formative memories. This is my log cabins and having a malted with my best girl at the soda fountain. This is my going to grandma's house and watching fireworks on the Fourth of July. This is my cherished childhood when crass consumerism and Hollywood blockbusters still meant something, dammit.

And now that I'm no longer a bitter child, but a *super bitter* adult, I keep thinking I might be done with *Star Wars*. But I'm always wrong. No amount of poor creative decisions, odd merchandising, or oversaturation seems to be able to crush the power of it.

So while I am perfectly capable of criticizing the quality of the films, making joke after *Star Wars* joke, and horrifying normal human beings with the depths of my *Star Wars* knowledge—did you know a Jedi must use the Force to place the Kaiburr crystal into the hilt of their lightsaber?—a part of me will always feel like I'm Luke Skywalker.

Like I'm a scrawny whiney farm boy staring off into the distance at the twin suns of Tatooine, supported by a bed of bittersweet, almost mournful music, as an empty box arrives in the mail.

As I open it, I am filled with a sense of destiny or, at the very least, hope.

GEEK TOPICS COVERED

- *Star Wars*
- Action Figures
- Yoda
- Zombies
- Legos
- Furries
- Hope

44

CONCLUSION OF DOOM

WELL, DEAR READERS, YOU HAVE NOW EXPERIENCED MOST OF MY BOOK.

At the risk of being overly conversational in prose form, here are some questions to help you process.

How was it for you? Did you have a good time? Did you die during the interactive fiction piece? Was it better, worse, or about the same entertainment value as the musical *Cats*? Did you make the robot farting noise with your mouth? Did you learn more about me than you really wanted to? Did you play the drinking game? Are you absolutely trashed right now?

Do you feel like there were some important geek topics that I missed? Of course you do. You're a geek.

In the introduction of the book, I described geeks as "intelligent, passionate people who have an open mind about becoming obsessed with something new."

I absolutely stick by that, but I think we all know there's a dark side.

All of us intelligent, open-minded geeks have an evil,

goateed, mirror-universe geek living inside us. It's the part of us that has a tendency to start sentences with the words "actually" or "technically." It's the part of us that gets really, truly annoyed when someone calls it *The Star Wars*, because, goddammit, there's no *The*! It's just *Star Wars*!

It's okay. I understand. I made the personal choice to skip a lot of geek subject matter. Personally, I wanted the book to deal with iconic topics, genres, and franchises that have real staying power. So I decided to leave out things like *Manimal* and *Heroes* and *Quantum LARPers* and *The Dragon Herders of Ithartak* and the cartoon *Battlestar Galactica Babies* and *Narnia: The New Testament* and George R. R. Martin's spin-off series *A Song of Hodor and Hodor* and the entire early 1980s Betamax punk aesthetic.

Only some of those things are real and some of the real ones are so sad and old, some people will think they're fake.

Regardless, I understand and sympathize with your desire to express what might be missing. On the following pages you will find two appendices. The first is a complete list of all Geek Topics Covered. The second leaves ample space for you to write in any important geeks topics you feel I missed.

I look forward to hearing about your additions to my book!

Thanks again for your purchase, borrowing, theft, or discovery in a time capsule of this book.

May The Living Long Force Stay With You While You Prosper and Don't Panic and Show People Your Boom Stick and Wait for Other Player so You Can Enter The Survival Horror and Shoot Some Dudez who Shall Not Pass and I'm Sorry About All Your Favorite Quotes I'm Leaving Out.

So say some, if not all of us.

Sincere thanks,

Joseph Scrimshaw
Writer/Comedian/Geek Flavored

GEEK TOPICS COVERED INDEX

3D Movies

Action Figures (x 2)
Adventure
Alcohol (x 4)
Allergies
Alternate Timelines
Anime
Angry Birds
Annoying Sidekicks (x 2)
Antilles, Wedge
Apocalypse, The
Astigmatism
Austen, Jane
Awkward Relationships (x 6)

Bacon
Batman (x 2)
Big Words (x 2)
Bizarro Superman
Blowing Things Up
Bond, James Bond (x 2)
Brains
Bunnies

Captain Kirk
Captain Picard
Cats
Cat Pictures
Catwoman
Collectible Trading Cards
Correcting People (x 3)
Cosplay
Couch's Ass Groove
Crafting
Cultists

Danger of Fantasy, The
Death Star, The
Demons
Dichotomies
Dickens, Charles (x 2)
Dinosaurs (x 2)
Doctor Who

Dodgeball
Double Rainbow
Dracula
Dungeons & Dragons
Dystopian Future

Eating
Emo
Emoticons
Explosions
Explosive Alcohol Adventures

FanFic
Fantasy (x 2)
Fez
Filking
Frozen Pizza (x 3)
Fruit Ninja
Fun
Furries

Goldeneye
Guilt
Guns

Halo
Harry Potter
He-Man
Highlander
Hipsters, Making Fun of
Hope (x 3)
Horror (x 2)
Horror of Reality, The (x 2)
Hugs
Hulk, The

IKEA
Interactive Fiction
Internet, The
Intrinsic Fallacy of Narrative Structure, The

Japanese Body Pillows
Jeopardy!

241

Kroffts, The

Lane, Lois
LARPing
Legos
Librarians
Lord of the Rings
Love (x 3)
Lovecraft, H.P. (x 2)

Mad Libs
Math
Mecha-Grandmother
Medical Conditions
Mummies
Muppets, The
My Geek Head
Myths

Ninjas (x 2)
Nintendo
Non-Euclidean Angles
Nudity

Online Comments
Online Gaming
Ordering Things from Amazon

Pac-Man
Pants (x 2)
Parties
Pizza Rolls
Pokémon
Ponies
Poor Rhyming Skills
Puppets

*Q*Bert*
Quantum Mechanics
Questionable Hygiene
Quoting Abraham Lincoln Incorrectly

Robin the Boy Wonder
Rule 34

Satan
Schrödinger's Cat
Science (x 2)
Sex
Sex, Doing
Slash Fiction

Sloth
Smartphones
Smoking Something
Social Media (x 2)
Space Robots
Spam
Special Days (x 2)
Special Feelings
Spider-Man
Spleen
Stabbing
Star Trek (x 3)
Star Wars (x 7)
Star Wars Prequels
Steampunk (x 2)
Superheroes (x 4)
Superman
Super Mario Bros.
Super Spies (x 2)
Super Villains (x 2)

Tacos
Teamwork
Tech Advice
TED Talks
Tentacles
Tetris
Time Travel (x 2)
Twilight

Ukulele

Vampires (x 2)
Vampire Ponies
Video Games (x 4)

War of the Worlds, The
Watching an Abusive Amount of Media (x 5)
Werewolves
Whedon, Joss
Wikipedia (x 2)

Xbox
X-Files, The
X-Men

Yankovic, Al
Yoda

Zeal
Zombies (x 3)

GEEK TOPICS MISSED

MY NAME	
GEEK TOPIC MISSED	

REASON GEEK TOPIC IS SIGNIFICANT:

MY NAME	
GEEK TOPIC MISSED	

REASON GEEK TOPIC IS SIGNIFICANT:

MY NAME	
GEEK TOPIC MISSED	

REASON GEEK TOPIC IS SIGNIFICANT:

MY NAME	
GEEK TOPIC MISSED	

REASON GEEK TOPIC IS SIGNIFICANT:

MY NAME	
GEEK TOPIC MISSED	

REASON GEEK TOPIC IS SIGNIFICANT:

MY NAME	
GEEK TOPIC MISSED	

REASON GEEK TOPIC IS SIGNIFICANT:

MY NAME	
GEEK TOPIC MISSED	

REASON GEEK TOPIC IS SIGNIFICANT:

MY NAME	
GEEK TOPIC MISSED	

REASON GEEK TOPIC IS SIGNIFICANT:

MY NAME	
GEEK TOPIC MISSED	
REASON GEEK TOPIC IS SIGNIFICANT:	

MY NAME	
GEEK TOPIC MISSED	
REASON GEEK TOPIC IS SIGNIFICANT:	

MY NAME	
GEEK TOPIC MISSED	
REASON GEEK TOPIC IS SIGNIFICANT:	

MY NAME	
GEEK TOPIC MISSED	
REASON GEEK TOPIC IS SIGNIFICANT:	

MY NAME	
GEEK TOPIC MISSED	
REASON GEEK TOPIC IS SIGNIFICANT:	

MY NAME	
GEEK TOPIC MISSED	
REASON GEEK TOPIC IS SIGNIFICANT:	

MY NAME	
GEEK TOPIC MISSED	
REASON GEEK TOPIC IS SIGNIFICANT:	

MY NAME	
GEEK TOPIC MISSED	
REASON GEEK TOPIC IS SIGNIFICANT:	

If more forms are needed, please contact Joseph at josephscrimshaw.com.

HALL OF GRATITUDE

This book was made possible by a Kickstarter campaign. Thank you to all the wonderful people listed below who pledged $10 or more to the creation of this book.

@aliceandstuff
Jo. Ackerman
Susan Adami
joel allan
Christopher Badell
daniel barnard
Glenn Basden
Andrew Beveridge
Jerry Bjelojac
Nicholas Bond
Enid Borgerding
Sandra Boyer
joseph bozic
Angela Brett
Tom Brincefield
Amelia Burger
Jon Caldwell
Joseph Camann
Kevin Carey
David Lars Chamberlain
Shane Charleson
Yves Claessens
Patrick Clapp
Rick Coleman
Colombe and Simcha
   (@cocodove and @simalot)
Cayenne Chris Conroy
Bill Corbett
A Jacob Cord
Paul Cornell
Caroline Craffigan
Shanan Custer
Yaron Davidson
Nick Decker

Daniel Deines
Gina Denn
Cole "The Magical Overlord of Pizza" Dilworth
Keith "One More MaiTai" Donaldson
Gary Dop
Meg Elliott
Jamas Enright
Zane Danger Evans
Francis & Adrienne Fernandez
JD Ferries-Rowe
Taylor & Maria Fisher
Brian "Fitz" Fitzpatrick
   (GameKnightReviews.com)
Fluffer McFancypants & Snoodles
Alex & Michelle Forte
Mona Fosheim Øwre
Robert Freeborn
Chris Friedlieb
Kyle Galer
Karl Geschwindt
Brett Glass
Susanne Goldmann
Bob Gorski
Andrew Hackard
Jerry R. Hall
Julia Haplo
Darrell Hardy
Pat Harrigan
J-D Harrington
Jason Hatrick
Jennifer Hayden

Elise Heise
Tom Hogan
Seth Crowbar Holloway
Kelly Hoolihan
Nicolas E Huaman
Birgit and Jens Humburg
Joshua Mark Humphrey
Conrad M. Hutcheson
Fellow Seamonkeys, Crickett & Phil Hutchinson
Steve Hutchison
Stacey Jaros
Craig Johnson
Dennis Zerwas, Jr.
Jennifer Kabacinski
Keshan Ken Jay
Lisa Kinney
Kisch & Mike
Greg & Stephanie Knepper
Niels Weiglin Knudsen
Reid Knuttila
Andrew Koehler
Edward Konarzewski
John Kovalic
Andy Kraft
Steve Krause
TJ & Amanda Kudalis
Misty Kuryliw
Renee Ladd
Sean Lake
Jessica Lamb
Ginny Landt
Kristi Lawless

247

Gary Leatherman	Brice Puls	Andy Stevenson
Michael Lee	William Rahn	Bill Stiteler
Lionheart	Mark J. Reed	Zach Stock
Creighton Long	Andrew Robbins	Jeremy Stomberg
Kristin Looney	David E Romm	Laura Sullivan
Curt Lund	Jason Roop	Scott Susser
Timothy Matson	Erin Root	Adam "8T" Tannir
Nicholas Mazzuca	Jason Ruvinsky	Jennifer Taylor
Heather Mbaye	Cathy Sandifer	Ben Thietje
Doug McBride	Jenn Schaal	Sandra Thornhill
Aric McKeown	Terri Lynn Schultz	Jim Tran
Courtney McLean	Jamie Schumacher	Alex Wareham
Bridget McManus	Jen Scott	Brian Watson-Jones
Mitchell and Michelle Melykson	Seamonkeys 1st Class Ben & Cynthia	Josh Way
Tim Mentzer	Ray Semiraglio	Will Weisert & Brenda Cornelius
Heather Meyer	Dr. Doug Shaw	Kathy Welch
Phillip Millman	Bryan Silverstein	Clarence Wethern
Adam Mirkovich	Gregory Skeels	Michael Wheeler
shean mohammed	Mike Skoglund	Tim Wick
Jack Moon	Amy Smith	Marcus Wilger
Keith "The Hammer" Nelson	Sharon Snyder	Alexandria Wilkie
nenegirl	Benjamin Soileau	C. Glen Williams
Laura Parcel	Michael Sphar	Eric Winn
Len Peralta	Jeff Spindler	Rob Withoff
rachel "piebob" perkins	Joyce Spirala	Christopher Wright
Shawn Pitre	Ryan Steans, Scourge of the Seven Seas	Sam Wright
Ben Powell	Eric Stephan	Jena Young
Sam Price	Courtney Stevens	Matilda T. ZombieQueen (Christine Malcom)

THANKS OF DOOM

I would first like to thank that person I am inevitably forgetting to thank in helping me make this book a reality.

To that person I say a statement that sums up almost all human interactions: thanks and sorry.

I would also like to give official credit to the following people.

Matthew Foster designed both the cover and the interior of the book. I want to say he did the interior design of the book but that makes it sound like he bought an ottoman and painted something mauve. He just did a kick-ass job working on all the design elements.

The multitalented **Craig VanDerSchaegen** helps me with my promotional photos, websites, and more. I sincerely hope that sixty years from now he will be the one helping me to scan my brain into a thumb drive so I can live forever inside the robot body he probably also built for me. For *Comedy of Doom,* Craig took the photo on the front cover.

The illustration on the back cover is the work of **Len Peralta**, creator and illustrator of the amazing *Geek-A-Week* trading card and podcast series. Len is a super-nice guy. The first time I met him in person, he let me finish a beer he didn't want to drink and our friendship has blossomed from there.

The illustration of the Honey Bear is by my good friend **Christopher Jones**, who is currently the artist on DC Comics' *Young Justice.* You should buy *Young Justice* to support Christopher and the possible appearance of the Honey Bear in a big battle scene.

John Kovalic, creator of *Dork Tower* and artist for countless games including *Munchkin* and *Apples to Apples,* provided the lovely artwork for "The Thing That Should Not Be Under Your Bed." John is a sweet, dear man. I'm very grateful that he let his dark sense of humor come out into the sun and play for my twisted Lovecraft story for kids. (John also gave me the story suggestion that eventually became "A Song of Rainbows and Also Rainbows." Thank or curse him as you feel is appropriate.)

My about-the-author photo was taken by **Dennis Zerwas, Jr.** during a live performance at the Bryant-Lake Bowl Theater in Minneapolis. I would like to compliment Dennis on his ability to get live performance photos of me in which it does not look like I'm fighting some form of facial paralysis.

I would also like to thank **Jody Wurl** and her mad librarian research skillz for tracking down valuable information about publishing *Comedy of Doom*.

The lovely and talented **Bill Stiteler** shot, directed, and edited the video for the book's Kickstarter campaign. Sadly, he refused my suggestion that he should make a Hitchcockian appearance in the video itself, so I thank him here.

Also, many thanks to all of the audiences and venues that supported the live show version of *Comedy of Doom*. The show premiered at a great convention in Minnesota called CONvergence. The show next played at the San Francisco Sketch Fest, and finally on Jonathan Coulton's JoCoCruiseCrazy. The gracious audiences on the cruise dubbed themselves Sea Monkeys so I get to write this: Thanks, **Sea Monkeys**.

Also, a special thanks to all involved in making those performances happen particularly **Mr. Coulton** as well as musicians, comedians, and all around awesome men Paul Sabourin and Greg DiCostanzo also known as **Paul and Storm**.

Yet another special thanks (not the same special thanks, a different one) to **Bill Corbett** and **Kevin Murphy** who have not only donated their time, talent, and support to the stage version of *Comedy of Doom,* they have also been known to buy me cocktails. I am honored to call them friends.

Many of the pieces in *Comedy of Doom* were developed while performing with a spoken word collective called the **Rockstar Storytellers** in the Twin Cities of Minneapolis and St. Paul. I thank them all for introducing me to the wide world of storytelling and giving me a place to experiment with creating a Frankenstein monster out of parts of storytelling and parts of stand up comedy.

Finally, thanks to **Sara Stevenson Scrimshaw** who said, "Hey, why don't you write a book?"

No vampire ponies were harmed in the making of this book.

This is the end of

Comedy of Doom,

but Joseph Scrimshaw will return in

TRAGEDY OF HOPE!

Made in the USA
Charleston, SC
05 July 2013